Contents

Happy Birthday, Lee!

Lee sent notes to his friends. The notes said,

It's my birthday!
Come to a party.
Where: 18 Elm Street
When: May 2 at 11:00
We'll have fun!
Lee

Dad baked a big cake for the party. It looked like a spaceship. He cooked hot dogs and buns on the grill. He made lemonade to drink.

Mom went to the store. She got chips to go with the hot dogs. She got ice cream to go with the cake.

Mom and Dad hung stars and moons in the backyard. They set the table with paper plates. They put party hats by the plates.

Lee's friends came to the party at 11:00. "Let's go into the backyard," said Lee. "We're going to play games."

After they played games, it was time to eat. "Come and get your hot dogs," called Lee's dad.

The hot dogs were good. Mike ate three of them. He ate a lot of chips. Then he drank a lot of lemonade. "You'll get sick, Mike," said Tami.

"I like hot dogs and lemonade," said Mike as he took a big drink.

"It's time for cake," called Lee's mom. Lee made a wish and blew out the candles. Lee and his friends ate ice cream with their cake.

Mike ate a lot of cake. He ate a lot of ice cream, too. "You'll get sick, Mike," said Maggie.

"I like cake and ice cream," said Mike as he took another bite.

Reading • EMC 4530 • ©2005 by Evan-Moor Corp.

Mom called, "Come on, Lee. It's time to open your presents."

Maggie gave Lee skates and Tami gave him a kite. Mike gave him a toy ape with a big hat. Then Mom and Dad gave Lee a green bike.

Lee hugged his mom and dad. "Thank you," said Lee. "I love my new bike! I can't wait to ride it."

"Thank you," Lee told his friends. "Come on. Let's play with them."

All of a sudden, Tami shouted, "Mike, you look green!"

"Oh!" moaned Mike. "I feel sick! I want to go home."

While Dad took Mike home, Lee and his friends played. They had fun with Lee's new toys all afternoon.

After You Read

Practice this page.
Make it sound like the people feel (happy, excited, sick).
Read the page to an adult.

Answer Questions about
Happy Birthday, Lee!

Fill in the circle or write the answer.

1. Why did Lee have a party?
   ○ It was Mike's birthday.
   ○ He was having a sleepover.
   ○ It was Lee's birthday.

2. Who came to Lee's party?

   _____

   _____

3. List Lee's presents.

   _____

   _____

4. Why did Mike get sick?
   ○ He was getting a cold.
   ○ He ate food that was bad.
   ○ He ate too much food.

5. Fill in the circle in front of the food the children ate at Lee's party.

   ○ birthday cake   ○ pizza   ○ chips

   ○ lemonade   ○ hot dogs   ○ soda

   ○ candy   ○ ice cream   ○ chicken

Reading • EMC 4530 • ©2005 by Evan-Moor Corp.

What Is It?

Find words in the story to name each picture.

_____

_____

_____

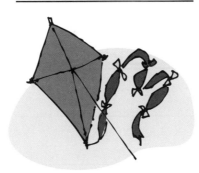

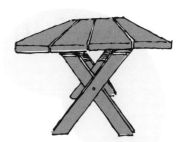

_____

_____

_____

_____

_____

_____

Mike

Write the sentences in order.

Mike got sick.

Mike ate a lot of cake.

Mike came to Lee's party.

Lee's dad took Mike home.

Mike ate three hot dogs.

1. <u>Mike came to Lee's party.</u>

2. _____

3. _____

4. _____

5. _____

Reading • EMC 4530 • ©2005 by Evan-Moor Corp.

Which Sound Do You Hear?

Write the words in the correct columns.

barn	map	sand	skate
candle	far	tape	plane
star	make	ran	card

a in **hat**	**a** in **cake**	**ar** in **car**
_____	_____	_____
_____	_____	_____
_____	_____	_____
_____	_____	_____

Write a sentence using one word from each column.

1. _____

2. _____

3. _____

A Word Family
old

Write **old** on the lines. Read the new words to an adult.

t <u>old</u>   c_____

f_____   h_____

m_____   s_____

Write the new words you made in these sentences.

1. I put on mittens when it is _____.

2. Can I _____ your puppy?

3. Mom _____ me to go to bed.

4. Will you help me _____ this blanket?

5. Dad _____ our old car.

6. There was _____ on the old bread.

Who Owns It?

We show that someone owns something by adding 's to his or her name.

Lee's skates.

Add 's to show who owns these things.

1. _____Dad's_____ grill
   Dad

2. _____ kite
   Lee

3. _____ hot dog
   Mike

4. _____ lemonade
   Tami

5. _____ party hat
   Maggie

6. _____ chips
   Mom

My Dog Max

My dog Max is a great dog. He can catch a rubber ball. He will fetch a stick when I throw it. He sits when I tell him to sit.

The only bad thing about Max is mud! He loves mud! If there is mud around, Max can find it. He plays in mud puddles after it rains. He rolls in wet dirt in the garden. I yell at Max. He just smiles at me.

When I got home from school today, Max was a mess. He had mud from his head to his tail. "Muddy Max, you are a mess," I said. His smile went away. Max knew that he was in trouble.

Reading • EMC 4530 • ©2005 by Evan-Moor Corp.

"Max," I said, "you need a bath."

Max hates getting a bath! As soon as I got the washtub and hose, Max took off. I chased him around the backyard. I chased him around the front yard. At last I grabbed him. Then I had to drag him to the tub.

"Get into the tub, Max," I said. Max just sat there.

"Come on, Max. Get into the tub!" I said. Max started to pull away.

"Oh, no you don't! You have to have a bath. You're a muddy mess!" I shouted.

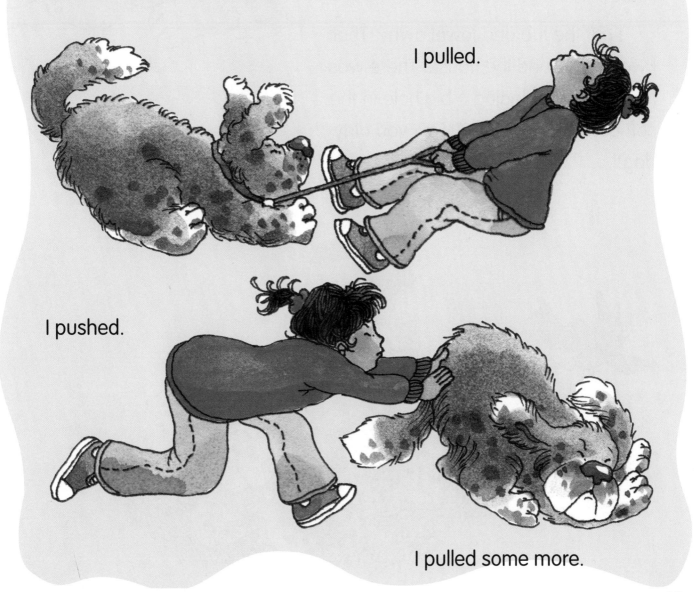

I pulled.

I pushed.

I pulled some more.

At last Max was in the tub.
I rubbed soap all over him. I got
the hose and rinsed off the soap.
I dried him with a big, old towel.
Max was fluffy and clean again.
"You look great, Max!" I told him.
"Now stay out of the mud."

Max licked my face. He ran off
wagging his tail. "What a good dog,"
I said.

I put the tub and towel away. Then
I walked around the house. There was
Max. He was digging a big hole in the
soft dirt in the garden. "Max, you dirty
dog!"

Reading • EMC 4530 • ©2005 by Evan-Moor Corp.

Answer Questions about
My Dog Max

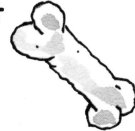

Fill in the circle or write the answer.

1. List three good things Max can do.

_____

_____

_____

2. What bad thing does Max do?

_____

3. How do you know that Max hates getting a bath?
   ○ He ran away.
   ○ He hid under the porch.
   ○ He rolled over and wagged his tail.

4. What did Max do after his bath?
   ○ He took a nap.
   ○ He dug in the dirt.
   ○ He ate his dinner.

Draw.

muddy Max	clean Max

Short Vowel Review

Color the boxes with short vowel words to help get Max to the tub for his bath.

a—an	**e**—egg	**i**—in	**o**—on	**u**—up

dog	and	I	ask	bath	yell
face	it	mud	when	out	soft
the	my	start	no	wag	his
box	as	fun	mess	catch	hose
will	smile	storm	need	water	dirt
Max	fetch	got	sit	run	tub

Reading • EMC 4530 • ©2005 by Evan-Moor Corp.

How to Give Your Dog a Bath

1	paste
2	paste
3	paste
4	paste
5	paste
6	paste

Put him in the water.

Wash the suds off the dog.

Dry him with the big towel and let him go.

Now catch your dog.

Fill a tub with water and get a big towel.

Rub the suds all over your dog.

What Does It Mean?

Match.

1. fetch   • a little pool of water

2. mud   • to get something and bring it back

3. puddle   • to use water to get soap off

4. drag   • wet dirt

5. rinse   • not hard

6. soft   • to pull

The Sounds of th

Circle the words with the sound of th in the.

Make an X on the words with the sound of th in three.

(then)	bath	that
there	throw	with
thimble	those	these

Adding Endings

	add **ed**	add **ing**
start	_____	_____
shout	_____	_____
pull	_____	_____
lick	_____	_____
paint	_____	_____

Read the new words to an adult.

Pronouns

Pronouns are words that take the place of nouns.

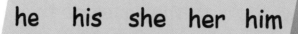

| he | his | she | her | him |

Write a pronoun on each line.

1. Jan has a great dog.

   She has a great dog.

2. Max can catch a ball.

   _____ can catch a ball.

3. Jan's dog was a muddy mess.

   _____ dog was a muddy mess.

4. Jan pushed and pulled Max.

   _____ pushed and pulled Max.

5. Jan gave Max a bath.

   _____ gave _____ a bath.

6. Jan put the tub and towel away.

   _____ put the tub and towel away.

7. Max was digging in the dirt.

   _____ was digging in the dirt.

8. Max licked Jan's face.

   _____ licked _____ face.

Reading • EMC 4530 • ©2005 by Evan-Moor Corp.

Five Furry Kittens

Five furry kittens one spring night
Sat on a fence. What a funny sight!

The first one danced
on her kitty toes.

The second one washed
his little black nose.

The third one turned
around and around.

The fourth one jumped
down to the ground.

The fifth one sang
a kitty song.

Five furry kittens
played all night long.

After You Read

Practice the poem.
When you can read it with no
mistakes, read it to an adult.

Answer Questions about
Five Furry Kittens

Fill in the circle or write the answer.

1. Where were the kittens sitting?

○ in a tree

○ on the ground

○ on the fence

2. What were the kittens doing?

first _____

fifth _____

second _____

fourth _____

third _____

3. Find the words in the poem that rhyme with these words.

sight _____

around _____

long _____

nose _____

Words That Mean the Same

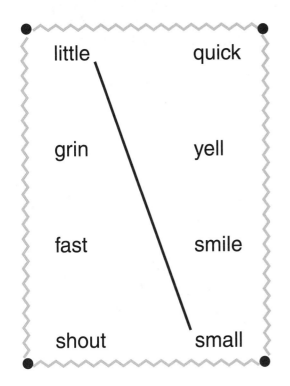

Match the words that mean the same.

little	quick
grin	yell
fast	smile
shout	small

middle	glad
happy	slow
pokey	center
large	big

Colorful Kittens

Color the kittens.

| first yellow | fourth gray | third black | fifth orange | second brown |

Camping

Hank called up his best friend Carlos. "My dad and I are going camping this weekend. Do you want to come with us? We can sleep in a tent and fish in the lake."

"That sounds like fun," said Carlos. "I'll pack my sleeping bag and fishing pole."

The next day, Dad and the boys set off for the woods. "There's a good spot for our tent and a campfire!" shouted Carlos.

It was an open space between a group of trees and the path to the lake.

The boys helped Dad set up two tents. They put their sleeping bags inside one of the tents. "You boys can find some firewood," said Hank's dad. "Then I'll make a campfire."

The boys went into the woods to find the firewood. Carlos found three long sticks. "We can use these to cook dinner," he told Hank.

Reading • EMC 4530 • ©2005 by Evan-Moor Corp.

Dad and the boys put hot dogs on the ends of the sticks and cooked them over the campfire. Then they cooked marshmallows over the fire. Everything tasted great!

After dinner the boys sat by the campfire. They sang songs and told funny jokes. Dad told a scary story.

It was getting dark. The sky filled with stars and a big, bright moon. It was getting cold, too. "Boy, this campfire feels good," said Hank. He moved closer to the fire to stay warm.

The boys could hear an owl hooting. They could hear something moving in the woods. "What was that?" asked Carlos.

"I don't know, but it sounds big," said Hank as he moved closer to his dad.

"I think we should go to bed now," said Carlos.

"Me, too!" agreed Hank.

The boys said good night to Dad. They went into the tent and shut the flap. Then they crawled into their sleeping bags. "I want to go fishing when I wake up," said Hank.

"I want to fish, too," said Carlos. "Good night, sleep tight, and don't let the bedbugs bite."

Soon both boys were asleep and dreaming about the big fish they would catch.

As soon as it was light, Dad called, "It's time to get up!"

When the boys were dressed, Dad said, "Look here." He pointed to a footprint in the dirt.

"I think that noise we heard last night was a deer," said Dad.

Both boys were hungry. "Let's fix breakfast," said Hank.

They put bread on their sticks and toasted it over the campfire. The toast was good with peanut butter and jam.

Then they took their fishing poles and ran down the path to the lake. "Let's see if we can catch lunch," said Carlos.

And they did!

Reading • EMC 4530 • ©2005 by Evan-Moor Corp.

Answer Questions about
Camping

Fill in the circle or write the answer.

1. Where were Dad and the boys going?
   - ○ to the beach
   - ○ to the woods
   - ○ to the desert

2. What were they going to do?
   - ○ sail a boat
   - ○ ride horses
   - ○ go fishing

3. Why did they need to collect firewood?

   _____

4. How did they cook their hot dogs and toast?

   _____

5. Why did the boys want to catch fish?
   - ○ to keep for pets
   - ○ to cook and eat them
   - ○ to take home to their moms

6. How do you think the boys felt when they heard something moving in the woods? Why?

   _____

   _____

What Is It?

Find words in the story to name the pictures.

_____   _____   _____

_____   _____   _____

<u>fishing pole</u>   _____   _____

What Happened Next?

Draw a picture to show what the boys did next.

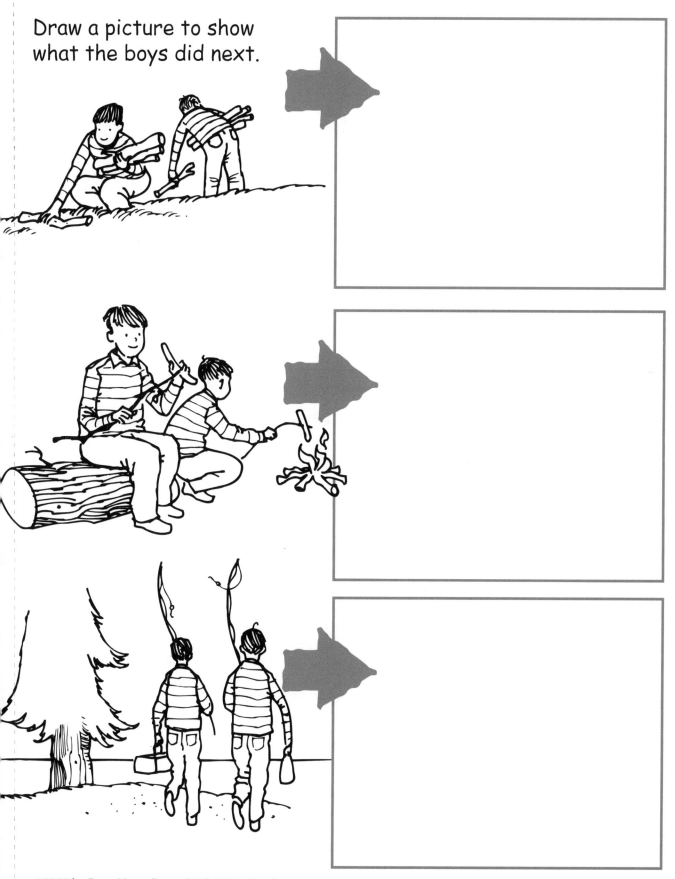

A Word Family
ick

st + ick = __stick__   p + ick = _____

l + ick = _____   k + ick = _____

s + ick = _____   ch + ick = _____

Use the new words you made in these sentences.

1. A baby _____ came out of its egg.

2. Carlos cooked his hot dog on a _____.

3. How far can you _____ the ball?

A Word Family
ead

h + ead = _____   d + ead = _____

r + ead = _____   br + ead = _____

l + ead = _____   spr + ead = _____

Use the new words you made in these sentences.

1. Hank _____ a story to his little sister.

2. He _____ butter on a slice of _____.

3. The clown had a funny hat on his _____.

The Sounds of ed

Read these words. Write them in the correct columns.

looked	wanted	filled
named	cooked	toasted
shouted	dreamed	picked

ed	d	t
___	___	___
___	___	___
___	___	___

Opposites

small   big

Match.

long	under
up	down
over	short

cold	come
go	happy
sad	hot

What Are You Doing?

Words that tell what you are doing are called verbs.

Draw a circle around the doing words (verbs).

(camping)	campfire	stars
sleeping	cooked	moving
scary	firewood	crawled
fishing	sang	good
funny	told	peanut butter
marshmallows	bright	dreaming

Reading • EMC 4530 • ©2005 by Evan-Moor Corp.

Peanut Butter

Do you like peanut butter? Jake loves it. He likes it on hot toast. He likes to eat it with a spoon. Most of all he likes peanut butter and jelly on bread.

One day Jake's mom took him to a peanut farm. The farmer said they could take some peanuts. Jake looked at the peanut plants, but he didn't see any peanuts. His mom said, "Peanuts grow under the ground."

They dug up some plants and picked the peanuts. "Thank you for the peanuts," Jake told the farmer.

On the way home, they stopped at the store. Jake's mom wanted to buy a jar of grape jelly. "Why are you buying jelly?" he asked.

"You'll see," was all she said.

When they got home, Jake took the peanuts out of their shells. His mom put the peanuts in a pan. She toasted them a little bit. Then she put the peanuts into the blender.

"Whir-r-r!" went the blender. The peanuts broke into little bits.

"Whir-r-r!" went the blender. The little bits got smoother and smoother.

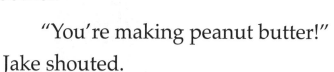

"You're making peanut butter!" Jake shouted.

Jake's mom got out some bread and the grape jelly. "I think it's time for a snack," she said with a smile.

"This is the best sandwich I ever had," Jake said. "May I have a glass of milk, too?"

Reading • EMC 4530 • ©2005 by Evan-Moor Corp.

Answer Questions about
Peanut Butter

Fill in the circle or write the answer.

1. Name three ways Jake likes to eat peanut butter.

_____

_____

_____

2. Where do peanuts grow?
   ○ on a tree
   ○ under the ground
   ○ under the water

3. Why did Jake's mom stop to buy grape jelly?
   ○ She needed it to make a pie.
   ○ She needed it to make a cake.
   ○ She needed it to make a sandwich.

4. How did Jake's mom make peanut butter?

_____

_____

_____

5. Do you like smooth peanut butter or chunky best? Why?

_____

_____

_____

What Does It Mean?

Match each word to its meaning.

1. toast
2. farm
3. blender
4. snack
5. sandwich
6. shell

• a place where crops are grown

• bread browned by heat

• the part of a peanut plant that holds the seeds

• two pieces of bread with meat, peanut butter, or another filling in between

• something to eat between meals

• a kitchen tool for grinding food into smaller pieces

Write the name of each picture.

_____   _____   _____

A Peanut Butter Sandwich

Number the sentences to show how to make a peanut butter sandwich.

_____ Cut the sandwich in half.

__1__ Get out the bread, peanut butter, jelly, and a knife.

_____ Put the slices of bread together.

_____ Put a lot of jelly on the other slice of bread.

_____ Sit down and eat it up!

_____ Open the jars of peanut butter and jelly.

_____ Put a lot of peanut butter on one slice of bread.

Make an **X** on the peanut butter sandwich you would like to eat.

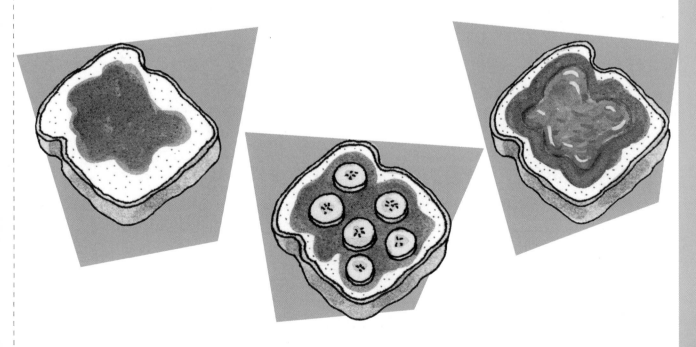

Long Vowel Sounds

Sometimes two letters together make the long sound.

ea—meat   **oa**—roast   ee—see

Write the missing letters to name the pictures.

c __oa__ t

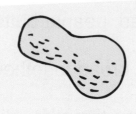

p_____nut

thr_____

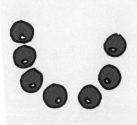

b_____ds

s_____ds

t_____st

Write the missing letters in each sentence.

1. I like to _____t ch_____se and m_____t sandwiches.

2. A funny g_____t rode on the circus fl_____t.

3. A bumbleb_____ flew by that tr_____.

Compound Words

Sometimes peanuts are called **groundnuts**. **Peanuts** and **groundnuts** are compound words. A compound word is two small words put together to make a new, longer word.

pea + **nut** = peanut	**ground** + **nut** = groundnut

Write the parts together to make new words.
Match the new words to the pictures.

rain + coat = _____

pan + cake = _____

sea + horse = _____

apple + sauce = _____

wind + mill = _____

Circle the two compound words in each sentence.

1. Did you know that peanuts grow underground?

2. The cowboy saw a rainbow in the sky.

3. A butterfly danced in the sunlight.

Alphabetical Order

When the first letter in each word is the same, look at the second letter.

Write the words in alphabetical order.

blender	**blender**
buy	**boy**
boy	**buy**

snack	_____
sandwich	_____
she	_____

peanut	_____
plant	_____
pick	_____

toast	_____
take	_____
time	_____

home	_____
his	_____
he	_____

jelly	_____
jar	_____
joke	_____

Jelly

Reading • EMC 4530 • ©2005 by Evan-Moor Corp.

The Case of the Missing Apples

Kate had a big, old apple tree in her backyard. The tree was covered with fruit. "My, those apples look good," she said. "They should be ripe in a few days."

Kate loved apples. She planned to make apple pies. "I think I'll make apple jelly, too," she said.

Every day, Kate looked at her fruit tree. Every day she saw more ripe apples. "I'll start picking them in the morning," she told her husband Frank.

In the morning, Kate went out to pick the apples. "Oh, no!" she cried. "Something has been eating my apples!"

Kate picked enough apples to make a pie. "I'll pick the rest of the apples tomorrow."

The next day, more apples were gone. Kate said, "I must find out what is eating my apples."

That night the moon was full. Kate took a blanket and went outside. She could see the apple tree in the moonlight. Kate wrapped up in her blanket and sat still and quiet. Kate watched the tree for a long time.

At last, Kate heard a noise. Something was moving in the apple tree. A furry face peeked out of the branches. Kate saw a long, pointy nose and big ears. It was a gray fox! The fox was carrying an apple in its mouth. "So you've been eating my apples!" Kate said.

Reading • EMC 4530 • ©2005 by Evan-Moor Corp.

When the fox heard Kate, it ran down the tree and scooted across the yard. Quick as a wink, the fox was gone.

Kate ran back into the house. "Frank! Frank! Wake up!" she shouted as she shook her husband.

Frank sat up in bed. "What's the matter?" he asked.

Kate told Frank what she had seen. "What are you going to do?" asked Frank. "How are you going to keep the fox out of your apples?"

The next day, Kate picked the ripe apples. She left a few apples for the fox. "I think we can share the apples," she said with a grin.

Answer Questions about
The Case of the Missing Apples

Fill in the circle or write the answer.

1. What made Kate unhappy when she went out to pick the apples?
   - ○ The apples were still green.
   - ○ The apples were all gone.
   - ○ Some apples had been eaten.

2. How did Kate find out what was taking the apples?
   - ○ She watched the tree all day.
   - ○ She stayed up all night to watch the tree.
   - ○ She called the police to find the thief.

3. Why do you think Kate needed a blanket?

   _____

4. What surprised Kate?

   _____

5. What does **quick as a wink** mean?

   _____

6. Why did Kate leave some apples on the tree?

   _____

7. What would you do if a fox was taking your apples? Why?

   _____

   _____

A Surprise in the Apple Tree

Cut out the sentences. Paste them in order.

1. | paste |

2. | paste |

3. | paste |

4. | paste |

5. | paste |

6. | paste |

Kate had an apple tree in her backyard.

Kate saw a fox in the apple tree.

Something was eating Kate's apples.

Kate picked the ripe apples. She left some for the fox.

The fox ran down the tree. It ran across the yard.

Kate sat in the moonlight. She watched the tree.

Opposites

Match.

inside	day	stand	long
night	husband	short	big
noisy	outside	frown	sit
wife	quiet	small	grin

Circle the two words in each sentence that are opposites.

1. Kate ran up and down the stairs.

2. I played all day and slept all night.

Reading • EMC 4530 • ©2005 by Evan-Moor Corp.

The Sounds of **gr** and **wr**

Fill in the missing letters. Read the new words you make to an adult.

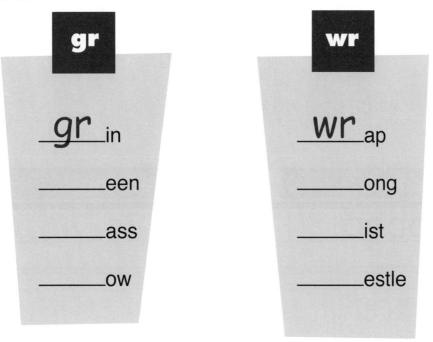

gr

__gr__ in

_____een

_____ass

_____ow

wr

__wr__ ap

_____ong

_____ist

_____estle

Use the new words you made to complete the sentences.

1. Kate started to gr_____ when she saw the fox.

2. Tom likes to wr_____ with his brother.

3. Dad asked me to mow the gr_____ gr_____.

4. Can you wr_____ this present for me?

Add Endings

In some words you must double the last letter before you add an ending.

> wrap + **p** + ing = wrapping
>
> wrap + **p** + ed = wrapped

add **ed**	add **ing**
grab **grabbed**	_____
brag _____	_____
rub _____	_____
wag _____	_____
plan _____	_____
rot _____	_____

Circle the correct word.

1. The dog _____ its tail.	wagged	wagging
2. He was _____ a party.	planned	planning
3. She _____ about her new bike.	bragged	bragging
4. The cat was _____ all the food.	grabbed	grabbing

Finish the Fox

Connect the dots to make one side of the fox's face.
Draw the other side and color the picture.

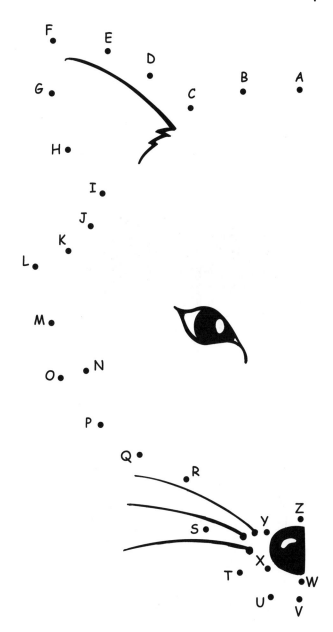

Write sentences telling what the fox looks like.

_____

_____

_____

May I Keep Her?

Nick went to the kitchen to get a glass of milk. He heard a noise. It sounded like scratching at the back door. He peeked out and saw a kitten. Nick called, "Mama, come see this!"

Mother picked up the wet kitten. She began to dry it with a towel. "You poor thing. You look like you've been lost for a long time."

It didn't have a collar. "Where do you belong?" she asked the kitten.

Nick looked at his mother and asked, "May I keep her?"

"We'll see in the morning," said Mother. "Now we're going to feed this skinny kitten. Then we'll put her to bed to get some rest."

Mother put an old blanket in a box. She put the box in the laundry room. Nick fed the kitten and put her in the box.

"Why can't she sleep in my room?" Nick asked.

"I know you would like that, Nick," said Mother. "But the kitten has fleas. You wouldn't want fleas in your bed. She'll be okay in here tonight."

Nick petted the kitten until it went to sleep. Then he went to bed.

Nick woke up in the middle of the night. He wanted to see the kitten. When he got to the laundry room, he heard the kitten. She was meowing. Nick went in and picked her up. He held her until they both went back to sleep.

In the morning, Mother had a big surprise! She found Nick and the kitten fast asleep on the floor.

When Nick woke up, he asked again, "May I keep her?"

"You can keep the kitten for now," Mother told Nick. "But someone may come looking for the lost kitten. You'll have to give her back. Can you do that?"

"Yes, I can," said Nick. "I'll take care of her now. But if her owner comes, I'll give her back."

Nick and his mother tried to find the kitten's owner. They put up signs in stores. They knocked on doors and asked, "Did you lose a kitten?" They put an ad in the newspaper. But no one came for the lost kitten.

Nick did take good care of the kitten. He fed her and gave her clean water. He played with her. He brushed her fur. The kitten grew bigger and stronger every day.

Many weeks passed. Still no one came for the kitten. One day Mother said, "She is your kitten now, Nick."

"I think I'll name you Tiger," said Nick. And he gave his kitten a big hug.

Answer Questions about
May I Keep Her?

Fill in the circle or write the answer.

1. What did Nick find when he opened the back door?
   ○ a wet black kitten
   ○ a wet yellow kitten
   ○ a wet white kitten

2. Name the three ways Nick and his mother tried to find the kitten's owners.

   _____

   _____

   _____

   _____

3. How did Nick take care of the kitten?

   _____

   _____

   _____

4. Circle the sentence in the story that shows:

   • that it had been raining

   • why Mother wouldn't let Nick take the kitten to bed with him

What Happened Next?

Pretend you are Nick. Write a letter to a friend. Tell your friend what happened after you heard the noise at the back door.

Dear _____,

_____

_____

_____

_____

_____

_____

_____

_____

Your friend,

Nick

What Does It Mean?

Match.

a band that goes around a pet's neck   skinny

where clothes are washed   kitchen

very thin   laundry room

a small insect that bites   collar

to hit hard with a fist   flea

a room where food is cooked   knock

Draw.

a wet cat	a blanket in a big box

The Sound of kn

The letters **kn** stand for the sound of **n** in words like **know** and **knock**.

Write **kn** on the lines. Read the new words you make to an adult. Match each word to its picture.

kn___ee

_____ot

_____ife

_____ight

_____it

Write sentences using two of the new words.

1. _____

2. _____

Contractions

Match.

we're	did not	wouldn't	I am
didn't	cannot	she'll	you will
we'll	we are	you'll	would not
can't	we will	I'm	she will

Now and Then

Write the words in the correct boxes.

hear	see	kept	knocked
knock	heard	keep	give
saw	play	gave	played

Now

hear

_____

_____

_____

_____

_____

Then

heard

_____

_____

_____

_____

_____

Listen for the Sound

Read the words.

night	Nick	skinny	give
kitten	it	light	tried
like	his	pick	with
I	Tiger	my	sign

Write each word in the correct box.

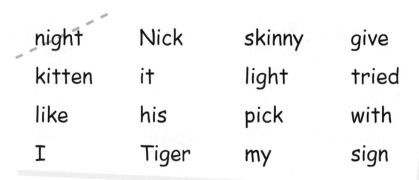

long i	short i
night	
_____	_____
_____	_____
_____	_____
_____	_____
_____	_____
_____	_____

Rashma's Nest

Rashma's bedroom was upstairs. A big tree grew outside her window. One branch of the tree almost touched her window.

One day, Rashma saw a robin making a nest in her tree.

- The robin used bits of twigs and weeds for the nest.

- The robin used mud to hold the nest together.

- The robin put grass in the nest to make it soft.

Soon the little nest was done. "It looks like a little brown cup sitting in my tree," thought Rashma.

The robin laid three small blue-green eggs in the nest. Day after day she sat on her eggs to keep them warm.

A few weeks later, Rashma heard a strange sound. It was coming from the tree outside her window. The eggs had hatched! Three tiny nestlings were in the nest. Their eyes were still closed. They had only a few fluffy feathers.

Rashma ran downstairs shouting, "The eggs hatched! Come see my baby birds!"

The new babies were very hungry and very noisy! The mother and father robin hunted for worms and insects. Back and forth they flew, feeding their hungry babies.

The babies grew bigger and bigger. They began to get feathers. They moved around the nest more. Soon they were flapping their wings. "I think the baby birds are getting ready to fly," said Rashma.

Rashma was right. One day the nest was empty. Her birds were gone! Rashma sat by the window feeling sad. While she sat there, the birds came back. They had not gone after all!

Rashma told her brother what she had seen. "You're right, Rashma," he said. "They're not ready to go yet. But soon they will fly away and not come back."

"I don't want them to go," said Rashma with a frown.

"I know. But they can't stay here all the time. They have to be off doing bird things," he said.

Rashma knew he was right. She looked up at her brother. "Do you think another robin will build a nest in my tree next year?" she asked.

Answer Questions about
Rashma's Nest

Fill in the circle or write the answer.

1. The robin was making a nest in _____.

   ○ a birdhouse

   ○ a hole in the ground

   ○ a tree

2. The nest was made of _____.

   ○ branches and leaves

   ○ twigs, weeds, and mud

   ○ grass and string

3. The robin sat on her eggs to _____

   _____.

4. The robins fed their nestlings _____

   _____.

5. Rashma felt _____
   when the birds flew away.

6. Rashma's brother told her that the birds _____

   _____

   _____.

Reading • EMC 4530 • ©2005 by Evan-Moor Corp.

A Robin's Life Cycle

Paste the pictures in order.

1
paste

2
paste

3
paste

4
paste

What Is It?

Find words in the story to name these pictures.

Silent e

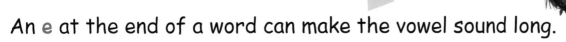

An e at the end of a word can make the vowel sound long.

can + **e** = cane   cub + **e** = cube

Add e to these words. Read the new words to an adult.

1. her   here   5. at   _____

2. bit   _____   6. tub _____

3. us   _____   7. kit _____

4. rob   _____   8. dim _____

Draw.

robe	kite	tube

More Than One

Add **s**. bird—birds		Change **y** to **i** and add **es**. cherry—cherries	
1. robin	_____	5. berry	_____
2. feather	_____	6. nest	_____
3. baby	_____	7. penny	_____
4. egg	_____	8. pony	_____

They or Them?   Write **they** or **them** on the line.

1. <u>Rashma and her brother</u> saw the birds.

   ___They___ saw the birds.

2. The robins fed worms to <u>the nestlings</u>.

   The robins fed worms to _____.

3. What did <u>the nestlings</u> look like?

   What did _____ look like?

4. Rashma didn't want <u>the birds</u> to go.

   Rashma didn't want _____ to go.

Hungry Nestlings

Draw three baby robins in a nest.
Draw the mother robin bringing a worm to the babies.

Write about the mother robin and her babies.

_____

_____

_____

_____

_____

Ten Little Monkeys

One little monkey swinging in a tree.

Two little monkeys splashing in the sea.

Three little monkeys playing on a swing.

Four little monkeys dancing in a ring.

Five little monkeys drinking lemonade.

Six little monkeys digging with a spade.

Seven little monkeys chasing furry cats.

Eight little monkeys wearing funny hats.

Nine little monkeys nodding little heads.

Ten little monkeys sleeping in their beds.

by Anonymous

Reading • EMC 4530 • ©2005 by Evan-Moor Corp.

Answer Questions about
Ten Little Monkeys

Fill in the circle or write the correct answer.

Write the correct number word.

1. How many monkeys were...

splashing in the sea? _____   wearing funny hats? _____

digging with a spade? _____   nodding little heads? _____

swinging in a tree? _____

2. What were seven monkeys doing?
   ○ nodding little heads
   ○ wearing funny hats
   ○ chasing furry cats

3. What were three monkeys doing?
   ○ sleeping in their beds
   ○ playing on a swing
   ○ swinging in a tree

Draw a monkey sleeping in this bed.

Find the Rhyme

Find two words in the poem that rhyme with each word.

1. bee   _____   _____

2. sleds   _____   _____

3. bring   _____   _____

4. rats   _____   _____

5. played   _____   _____

What Is It?

Find a word in the poem to name each picture.

_____   _____   _____

Write the number words.

_____   _____   _____

Reading • EMC 4530 • ©2005 by Evan-Moor Corp.

Pancakes Every Sunday

Nell sat up in bed. She heard a sound coming from the kitchen. Pa was singing. Nell jumped out of bed. "Today is pancake day!" she said.

Pa always made pancakes on Sunday. He made them just the way Nell liked them.

Nell put jam on her pancakes. Ma and Grandma put hot syrup on their pancakes. Pa ate his with bacon.

Nell got dressed and ran to the kitchen. She knew there was work to do. "Pa likes me to help," she said to herself.

Pa always told her, "You're the best cook's helper I've ever had."

Pa tied a towel around Nell. This was her apron. He grinned at Nell and said, "Let's cook!"

Pa let Nell help make the pancake batter. She measured the milk and poured it into the bowl. Pa stirred the batter to mix in the milk. Nell broke an egg into the batter. Pa stirred some more.

At last the batter was ready. Pa poured it on a hot griddle. Nell watched the pancakes. When she saw bubbles all over the pancakes, she called Pa. He flipped the pancakes over. Now they could cook on the other side. Soon they were golden brown. Pa put the pancakes on plates.

While they ate the pancakes, Pa kept cooking. He was good at eating and cooking at the same time! Pa made pancakes until everyone was full.

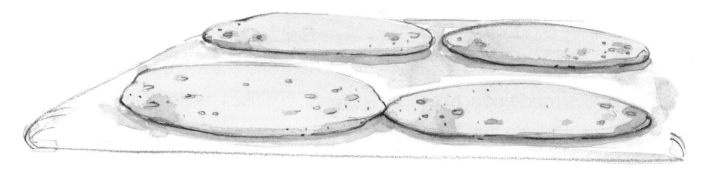

Reading • EMC 4530 • ©2005 by Evan-Moor Corp.

After the last tasty bite, Ma smiled. She said, "Those were the best pancakes you've ever made!"

Grandma said, "I'm so full I think I'm going to pop!"

And Nell said, "May I have one more?"

Today Grandma ate one pancake. Ma ate two pancakes. Pa ate three pancakes.

But Nell was really hungry. She ate four! When she asked for one more, Ma frowned. "Don't you think you've had plenty?" she asked.

Pa just laughed. He said, "A growing girl needs her food." He made one more pancake for his cook's helper.

Answer Questions about

Pancakes Every Sunday

Fill in the circle or write the answer.

1. What happened every Sunday at Nell's house?
   ○ Grandma made waffles.
   ○ Ma made pancakes.
   ○ Pa made pancakes.

2. What did each person like on their pancakes?

   Grandma and Ma _____

   Pa _____

   Nell _____

3. Tell three things that Nell did to help Pa make pancakes.

   _____

   _____

   _____

4. What did the bubbles on top of the pancakes mean?
   ○ It was time to turn the pancakes over.
   ○ It was time to eat the pancakes.
   ○ It was time to pour syrup on the pancakes.

Nell's Sunday Morning

Read the sentences about Nell.
Number them in order.

_____ Nell ate four pancakes.

__1__ Nell jumped out of bed.

_____ Nell helped make the batter.

_____ Nell asked for one more pancake.

_____ Nell watched for bubbles on the pancakes.

_____ Nell ran to the kitchen.

Number the pictures in order.

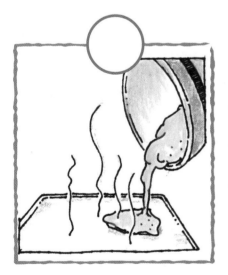  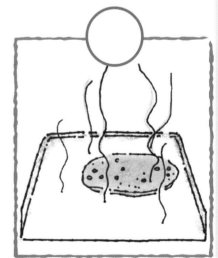

A Pancake Crossword Puzzle

Word Box

cook	flipped	griddle	pancakes
Sunday	syrup	whole	

Across ————————————

3. to make something to eat
4. a heavy, flat pan used to cook pancakes
5. thin, flat cakes
7. a day of the week

Down ————————————

1. all of something
2. turned over
6. a thick, sweet liquid

Reading • EMC 4530 • ©2005 by Evan-Moor Corp.

The Sounds of oo

The letters oo have more than one sound.
Write the words in the correct columns.

~~book~~	zoo	school	stood
crook	goose	soon	good-bye
boot	hoop	hood	moon
foot	cookie	good	balloon
	look	too	

oo in cook

book

_____   _____   _____

_____   _____   _____

_____   _____   _____

oo in food

_____   _____   _____

_____   _____   _____

_____   _____   _____

Add an Ending

Words that end with the letter **e** must be changed when you add the ending **ing**.

drop the **e** and add **ing**
rac**e**   rac**ing**

Add **ing** to these words.

1. bake _____   4. measure _____

2. smile _____   5. sprinkle _____

3. bite _____   6. pour _____

Use the new words you made to complete these sentences.

1. Pa is _____ at Nell.

2. Nell is _____ the milk.

3. Ma is _____ syrup on her pancakes.

Contractions

In these contractions **n't** stands for **not**.
Write the meaning for each contraction.

1. isn't _____   3. don't _____

2. wouldn't _____   4. hasn't _____

          Reading • EMC 4530 • ©2005 by Evan-Moor Corp.

Pancake Toppers

Unscramble the words to name each picture.
Make an X on each thing you would put on your pancakes.

terbut

surpy

amj

b _ _ _ _ _

_ _ _ _ _

_ _ _

anaban

snut

yhone

_ _ _ _ _ _

_ _ _ _

_ _ _ _ _

Draw your pancakes here.

Row Your Boat

Will lived in a big house on a farm near a river. He lived there with his mother and father. Will didn't have a brother or a sister. But he did have plenty of pets.

Will looked out the front window one summer day. The sun shone down. White clouds floated in the blue sky. A soft breeze blew leaves on the trees. "I think I'll go to the river and row my boat," he said.

"All right, Will," said his mother, "but stay near the riverbank."

"I will," shouted Will as he ran out the door.

When he reached the river, Will pushed his rowboat into the water. Quick as could be, he was in the rowboat. Soon he was rowing down the river. As he rowed he sang, "I row, row, row my boat."

Will didn't see his dog running along the riverbank.

All of a sudden, the boat began to rock. Will's dog had jumped into the boat and licked Will's face. "Down, boy!" said Will. "Don't rock the boat!"

The dog lay down by his feet. Will began to row the boat again.

Will didn't see his cat sitting in a tree that grew by the riverbank.

Again Will felt the boat rock. A furry shape landed in his lap. It was the cat! His dog jumped up and started to bark. Will said, "Be still, Cat! Be still, Dog! Don't make me drop my oars!"

The cat sat down in the back of the rowboat. She began to purr. The dog stopped barking and sat by Will's feet. Will started to row the boat again. He sang, "I row, row, row my boat."

Will didn't spy the duck flying overhead.

Will had gone only a few yards when he heard, "Quack! Quack!"

Down flew his pet duck, landing on Will's head. The dog began to bark and the cat began to yowl. "Sit down!" shouted Will. And he pushed the duck off his head.

The duck sat down at the front of the boat. The dog and cat sat down quietly. Will picked up the oars and began to row. "This boat is getting pretty full," he thought.

"I row, row, row my boat," sang Will as he and his pets floated along. The animals were quiet. The warm sun shone down. The water was smooth. "What a nice way to spend a summer day," he said to his pets.

Will didn't notice the fat pig and nanny goat standing on the riverbank.

"What now?" Will shouted, as his pet pig jumped into the middle of the boat. The dog barked and the cat yowled. The duck flapped its wings and quacked.

"This has got to stop!" shouted Will. He pushed the pig under his seat.

When the animals were still and quiet, Will picked up his oars. Before the oars could touch the water, four feet landed in the boat! It was Will's pet goat. This was too much!

The animals were making a terrible noise. The boat was so heavy now that water splashed over the sides. The cat, which hated water, jumped onto Will's shoulders.

"Oh, no! We're going to sink!" shouted Will.

When the other animals heard this, they jumped over the side. The dog, duck, pig, and goat all swam to the riverbank.

With the animals gone, the boat rose back up in the water. "I guess we won't sink after all," said Will to the cat. And off they rowed together. The cat purred and Will sang, "I row, row, row my boat."

Answer Questions about
Row Your Boat

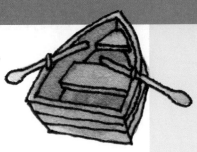

Fill in the circle or write the answer.

1. What did Will do on the fine summer day?

   ○ went for a walk   ○ went for a swim   ○ went for a boat ride

2. List the animals that jumped into the rowboat.

   _____

   _____

3. What did the dog do every time a new animal jumped into the boat?

   ○ began to cry   ○ began to meow   ○ began to bark

4. Why did water begin to come into the boat?

   ○ because there was a hole in the boat

   ○ because the boat was too full

   ○ because it started to rain

5. Which animal landed

   in the middle of the boat? _____

   in Will's lap? _____

   on Will's head? _____

6. Why do you think Mother told Will to stay near the riverbank?

   _____

   _____

What Happened Next?

Number the pictures in order.

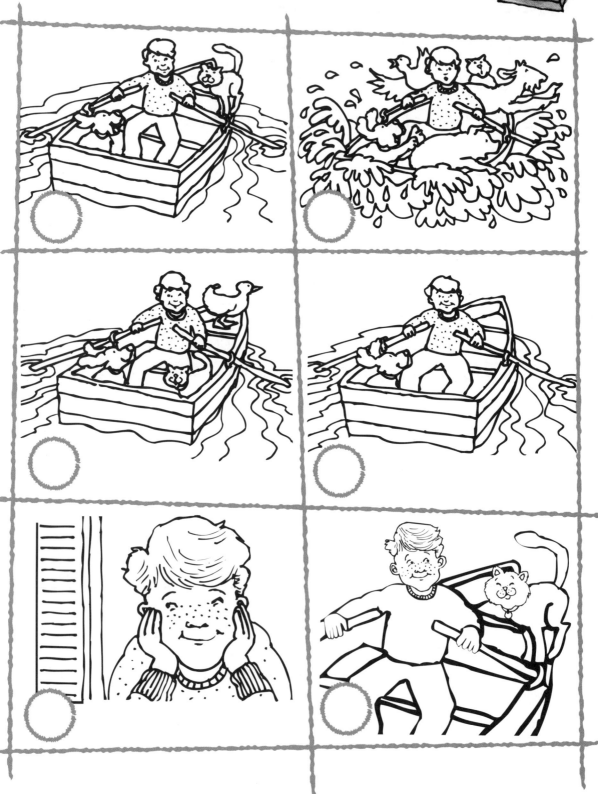

What Does It Mean?

Use these words to complete the sentences below.

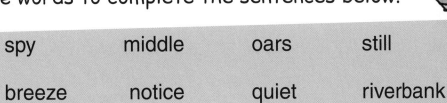

spy	middle	oars	still
breeze	notice	quiet	riverbank

1. Will used _____ to row the boat.

2. Trees were growing along the _____ .

3. _____ and _____ are two other words that mean **see**.

4. A big seed was in the _____ of the peach.

5. A soft _____ was blowing the leaves on the trees.

6. You must be _____ and _____ while you rest.

Farm Animals   Find these animals in the word search.

cat   hen

cow   horse

dog   lamb

duck   pig

goat   rooster

goose   sheep

g o o s e w t r
h r d u c k p o
o c z c o w i o
r a g o a t g s
s t m h e n t t
e s d o g x n e
q v l a m b o r
s h e e p b o x

What Sound Do You Hear?

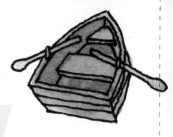

Write the words in the correct columns.

row	house	show
down	know	brown
cloud	yowl	grow
flow	sound	below

sound of **ow** in **cow**	sound of **o** in **go**

_____ _____   _____ _____

_____ _____   _____ _____

_____ _____   _____ _____

Fill in the missing letters to name the pictures.

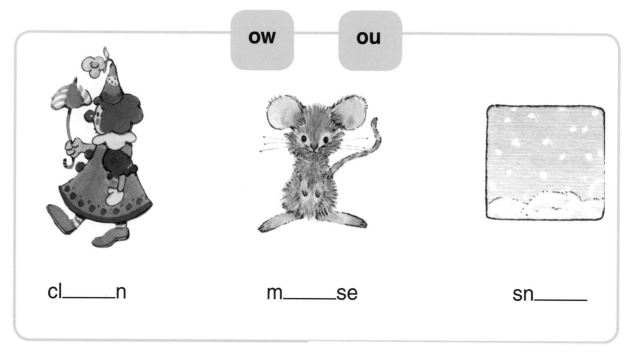

ow	ou

cl____n   m____se   sn____

A Word Family
oat

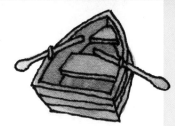

Write **oat** on each line. Draw a picture of the word you make.

b_____

g_____

c_____

fl_____

Write a sentence using each word you made.

1. _____

2. _____

3. _____

4. _____

Sail, Sail, Sail Your Boat

You can make your own boat to sail in a tub of water. Just read and follow each step.

You will need to get these things:
- a small milk carton
- a 4-inch square of heavy paper
- an ice-cream stick
- a small lump of clay
- glue

1. Cut off one side of the milk carton.

2. Put a lump of clay in the bottom of the boat.

3. Glue the sail to the ice-cream stick.

4. Stick the ice-cream stick into the clay.

5. Put your boat in a tub of water.

6. Blow into the sail to make the boat move.

How many small toy animals can you put into your boat before it sinks? _____

After You Read

Practice this page.
When you can read it with no mistakes, read it to an adult.

90

The Ugly Duckling

In the country far from town, there was a large pond. It was in the middle of a field. The field was near a big farm. Many ducks and geese lived by the pond. Hidden in the reeds and grass was a nest of eggs. It was the nest of a mother duck.

Day after day, Mother Duck sat on the eggs. She was waiting for them to hatch. As she turned her eggs each day, she would stop at one egg. It was much larger than the other eggs in the nest. Mother Duck would think, "What will this duckling be like?"

One day Mother Duck heard a pecking sound. Then she heard, "Peep! Peep! Peep!" The ducklings were coming out of their shells!

One by one, Mother Duck saw her fluffy yellow ducklings hatch. But she shook her head and frowned when the last one hatched. He was big. He was gray. And he was ugly.

"Oh, my! What an ugly duckling," was all Mother Duck could say.

Mother Duck loved all of her ducklings. She took good care of them, too. She took them to the pond to swim. She helped them find food. She showed them how to hide from danger.

Soon the days began to get colder. Mother Duck took her ducklings to the barn. There they would stay warm.

Reading • EMC 4530 • ©2005 by Evan-Moor Corp.

The other animals in the barn were unkind to the ugly duckling. They laughed at him and called him names. They even pecked at him. Mother Duck tried to protect her big, gray duckling, but she wasn't always around.

Ugly Duckling couldn't stand the teasing any longer. He ran away from the barn. He ran from the farm animals. And he ran from his family. He ran on and on until he came to a big lake.

Ugly Duckling felt safe at the lake, but he was lonely. None of the wild ducks would talk to him. One day, the duckling looked up into the sky. He saw a beautiful swan flying by. He looked into the water of the pond. All he saw was a big, gray ugly duckling. "I wish I were beautiful like that swan," he said softly.

It was getting colder. Ugly Duckling saw the wild ducks fly away. Soon ice covered the lake. Ugly Duckling was always cold. He didn't have much food to eat. Would he be able to stay alive until spring? He knew he had to find a warm place to stay.

Ugly Duckling looked around until he found an old shed. In the shed he found hay that had been left behind. Ugly Duckling made a nest out of the hay. Now he would be warm. He found some dry seeds, too. Now he would have a little bit to eat.

Ugly Duckling stayed in the shed all winter. He only went out into the cold winter weather to find water to drink.

At last spring arrived. Ugly Duckling was still alive! The days grew warmer. The ice covering the pond melted. The duckling found plenty to eat. Each day he grew bigger and stronger.

One day, as he stretched his wings, he was lifted up into the blue sky. He was flying! He flew over green fields. He flew over tall trees. He flew back to the pond where he had been born.

Ugly Duckling landed on the water and swam around. He looked down into the water to find something to eat. He couldn't believe his eyes! Over the winter, he had grown up. He wasn't an ugly duckling anymore.

The animals from the farm came down to the pond. They were surprised to see the large white swan. No one knew that the beautiful swan had been the ugly duckling they treated so unkindly.

After You Read

Practice this page.
Make it sound exciting.
Read it to an adult.

Answer Questions about
The Ugly Duckling

Fill in the circle or write the answer.

1. Why was the duckling called ugly?

  ○ He was big and yellow, not small and yellow.

  ○ He was small and gray, not small and yellow.

  ○ He was big and gray, not small and yellow.

2. Write three ways Mother Duck took care of her ducklings.

_____

_____

_____

3. Why did the Ugly Duckling run away from the farm?

  ○ He wanted to see new places.

  ○ He wanted to get away from the farm animals.

  ○ He wanted to find some swans.

4. Where did the Ugly Duckling spend the winter?

  ○ He stayed in the lake.

  ○ He hid under a tree.

  ○ He hid in an old shed.

5. How did the Ugly Duckling change over the winter?

_____

Reading • EMC 4530 • ©2005 by Evan-Moor Corp.

What Happened Next?

Cut out the sentences. Paste them in order.

1. paste

2. paste

3. paste

4. paste

5. paste

When winter came, the Ugly Duckling found an old shed to live in.

The farm animals called the Ugly Duckling names and pecked at him.

Mother Duck sat on her eggs. At last they hatched. One duckling was big and gray and ugly.

Over the winter, the Ugly Duckling grew up. He wasn't a duck! He was a beautiful swan.

The Ugly Duckling ran away. He ran until he came to a lake.

What Does It Mean?

Write each word after its meaning.
You will not use all of the words.

duckling	hatch	shed	tease
frown	lake	swan	winter

1. a small building used to store things _____

2. to treat others in an unkind way _____

3. to break out of an egg _____

4. a large body of water surrounded by land _____

5. an unhappy look on someone's face _____

Long Vowel Sounds

Write the words under the long vowel sound you hear.

they	sigh	cold	find
no	he	lake	fly
stay	tease	ice	ate
see	float	row	mean

a—cake	**e**—me	**i**—kite	**o**—go
_____	_____	_____	_____
_____	_____	_____	_____
_____	_____	_____	_____
_____	_____	_____	_____

It Sounds Like er

Read the words.
Circle the letters that make the **er** sound.

dirt	her	turn	butter
first	stir	hurt	after

Opposites

Match each word to its opposite.

large	smile	none	cry
frown	sad	went	go
beautiful	full	laugh	hot
happy	small	stop	came
empty	ugly	cold	all

~~~~~ **Add an Ending** ~~~~~

Add **ed.**

land_____   peck_____   hunt_____

protect_____   turn_____   jump_____

whisper_____   look_____   want_____

Circle the words where **ed** has the sound of **t.**

Make an **X** on words where **ed** has the sound of **d.**

Read the new words to an adult.

A Swimming Swan

Follow the steps to draw a swan on the lake.

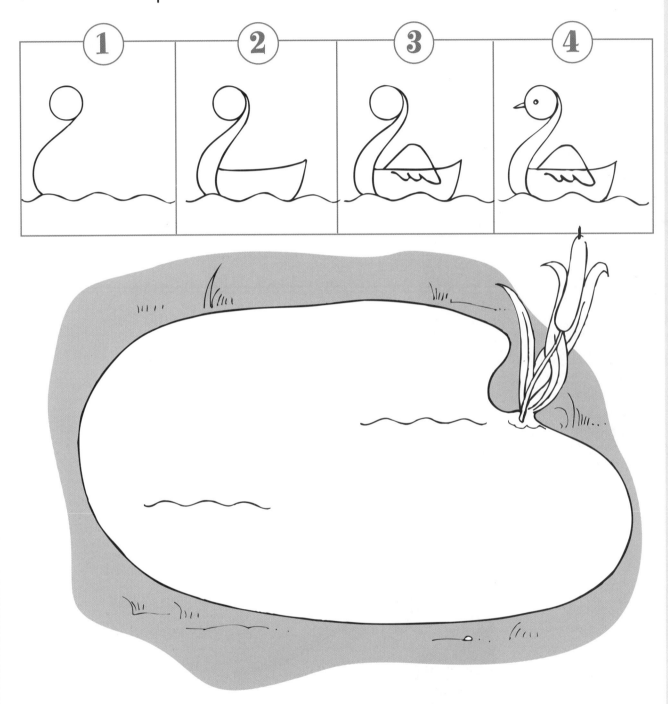

Write an interesting sentence telling what the swan is doing.

_____

_____

Elephants

Elephants are big! They are the biggest animals that live on land. They have long noses called trunks. They have big ears that can flap like fans. Their skin is gray-black. They have some short hairs on their backs and tails.

Bulls live alone or in small groups. Cows live in herds with their calves.

What Elephants Eat

Elephants must eat most of the day to get the amount of food they need. They eat grasses and shrubs. They eat twigs, leaves, and bark from trees.

An elephant must drink many gallons of water, too.

Reading • EMC 4530 • ©2005 by Evan-Moor Corp.

An Elephant's Trunk

An elephant's trunk has many uses. It is used to pick up food. Then the food is put into the elephant's mouth. An elephant drinks by sucking up water into its trunk. Then the elephant squirts the water into its mouth.

Elephants use their trunks to greet one another. They hold their trunks high to catch smells in the air.

The whole trunk is so strong it can rip a branch off a tree. The tip of the trunk can pick one berry off a bush.

**Asia
(A´zhuh)**

**Africa
(Af´rih kuh)**

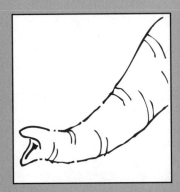

The trunk of an elephant from Asia has one lip on the tip of its trunk.

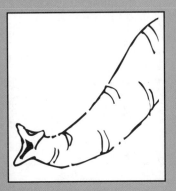

The trunk of an elephant from Africa has two lips on the tip of its trunk.

Elephant Babies

An elephant baby is very big. It weighs more than a grown human. The newborn calf sucks milk from its mother. The mother will feed her baby for two years. After a few months, the baby will also eat plants.

Where Elephants Live

Elephants live in Africa and Asia. They live on grasslands and in forests.

An elephant from Asia is smaller. It has smaller ears.

An elephant from Africa is larger than one from Asia. It has bigger ears.

Answer Questions about
Elephants

Fill in the circle or write the answer.

1. What does an elephant look like?

   _____

   _____

2. Which elephants live in herds?
   - ○ bulls and cows
   - ○ cows and calves
   - ○ bulls and calves

3. Name two places elephants live.

   _____

4. How do elephants get their food?

   _____

   _____

   _____

5. How else do elephants use their trunk?

   _____

   _____

   _____

Elephant Parade

Write the correct number under each elephant.

| third | eighth | seventh | sixth | first |
| second | fourth | fifth | tenth | ninth |

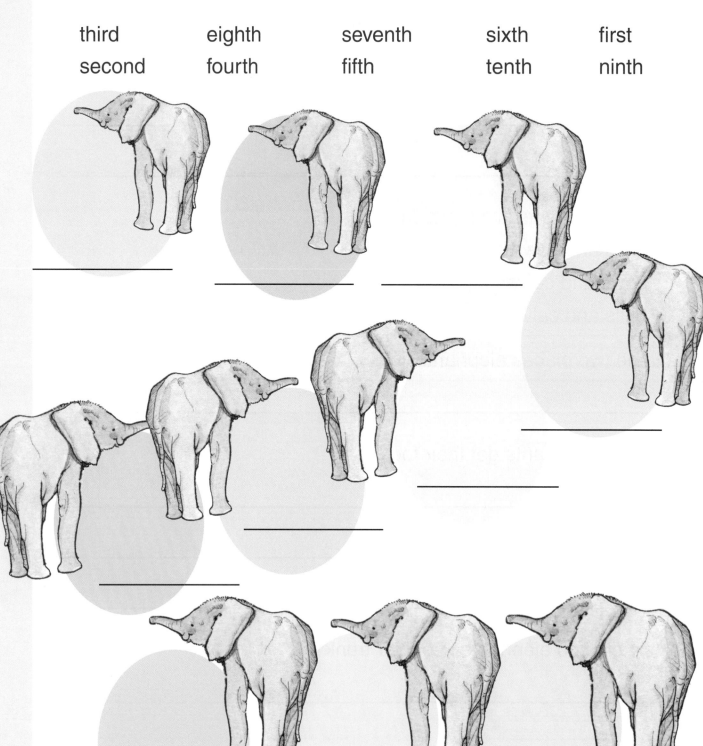

_____

_____   _____

_____

_____

_____

_____

_____   _____

_____

Find the Right Word

Fill in the missing word in each sentence.
You will not use all of the words.

tip	bark	Africa	twigs
bull	cow	calf	Asia

1. An elephant picks berries with the _____ of its trunk.

2. A _____ is a baby elephant.

3. A _____ is a mother elephant.

4. Elephants eat _____ and _____ from trees.

5. Elephants live in _____ and _____.

Write the meaning of the word **trunk** in each sentence.

1. The squirrel hid nuts in a hole in the tree's **trunk**.

    Trunk means _____.

2. An elephant picked berries with its **trunk**.

    Trunk means _____.

A Word Family

ay

All the words in a word family end with the same letters and sound. Write **ay** after each letter to make a word family.

d_ay___   h_____   st_____

l_____   b_____   pl_____

m_____   p_____   gr_____

r_____   w_____   cl_____

Read the word family aloud to an adult.

Ways to Spell /ā/

Underline the words that have the sound of **a** in **may**.
Circle the letters that make the **a** sound.

weigh   gray   they   parts

tail   Asia   water   baby

More Than One

Add an ending to make each word mean **more than one**.

Add **s**	Add **es**	Change **y** to **i** and add **es**
tree tree**s**	dish dish**es**	cherry cherr**ies**

1. tail _____

2. bench _____

3. lady _____

4. leg _____

5. baby _____

6. berry _____

7. ear _____

8. wish _____

9. fox _____

10. egg _____

A calf is one baby elephant. What word in the story names

more than one calf? _____

Little Lost Elephant

Help the lost elephant calf find its mother.
Color the boxes with words that rhyme with **too** to make a path.

moo	two	do	moon	what
door	soon	new	week	barn
calf	her	shoe	walk	they
water	bull	blue	flew	mine
spoon	twig	live	who	cow
trunk	berry	herd	knew	clue

How
BEAR
Lost His
TAIL

Long, long ago bears had handsome, bushy tails. But that all changed one winter. This is what happened.

Bear had a long, furry tail. He was very proud of his tail. He was always showing it off to the other animals.

Bear would wave his tail around and ask, "Can you see my tail? Don't you think it is the most handsome tail you've ever seen?"

The other animals thought Bear was too proud. After all, many animals had nice, long tails. But they were afraid to make Bear angry. He did have those powerful paws. And each paw had sharp claws. An angry bear could be very scary. So the animals would say, "Yes, you have the best tail."

One cold winter's day, Bear went looking for something to eat. He was walking along the river when he saw Fox. Fox was sitting on the ice by a pile of fish.

Fox thought, "Bear is too proud of that tail of his. He needs to be taught a lesson. I think I'll play a trick on him."

The clever fox knew that Bear was hungry. "Hello, Bear," he said.

"Hello, Fox," Bear said as he looked at Fox's fish. "Where did you get all of those fish?"

"I caught them in the river," said Fox.

Bear couldn't see a fishing pole. He asked, "What did you use to catch them?"

"I use my tail," said Fox. "I drop it into the hole in the ice. When a fish grabs my tail, I pull it out and the fish comes, too."

Bear had never heard of fishing that way. But there was Fox with all of the fish he had caught. Bear thought about how good fish would taste. "I didn't know you could fish that way. Maybe I'll try it. I would like some tasty fish for lunch."

Bear was sure that he would catch many more fish than Fox. After all, his tail was much longer. Fox watched as Bear found a spot on the ice. Bear used his sharp claws to dig a hole.

"Now you must sit down with your back to the hole," explained Fox. "Then drop your handsome tail into the water. When you feel a fish bite, quickly pull out your tail. The fish will be caught."

Bear's stomach began to rumble. He was very hungry. Bear sat down and dropped his tail into the water.

Fox said, "You must sit very still or you will scare the fish away." Then Fox picked up his own fish. He walked away, laughing at the foolish Bear.

Bear sat and waited for a fish to bite his tail. He thought about all of the fish he would catch. He sat still for so long that he fell asleep.

While Bear slept, it grew colder. Soon the hole in the water froze shut.

When Bear woke up he felt something holding his tail. Bear thought it was a fish. He jumped up and tried to pull his tail out of the water. But his tail did not move. The frozen tail broke off. All that was left of his handsome tail was a small stump!

"My tail! My tail is gone!" cried Bear. The once proud bear had no tail and no fish. He slowly walked back to his den, hanging his head in shame.

And that is why to this day bears have short tails.

After You Read

Practice this page.
Think about how Bear will sound.
When you are ready, read it to an adult.

Reading • EMC 4530 • ©2005 by Evan-Moor Corp.

Answer Questions about

How **BEAR** Lost His **TAIL**

Fill in the circle or write the answer.

1. Why was Bear so proud of his tail?
   ○ It had brown and white stripes.
   ○ It was long and furry.
   ○ It was short and curly.

2. Why were the animals afraid to make Bear angry?

   _____

3. How did the clever fox trick Bear?

   _____

   _____

   _____

4. What happened to Bear's long tail?
   ○ It grew longer and longer.
   ○ It froze and broke off.
   ○ The fish ate Bear's tail off.

Draw Bear with a long, handsome, bushy tail.	Draw Bear with a short stump of a tail.

What Happened Next?

Draw what happened next.

As Bear was looking for something to eat, he passed the river.

What happened next?

Fox told Bear he had caught fish by putting his tail in a hole in the ice.

What happened next?

Bear fell asleep with his tail in the water. The water froze.

What happened next?

What Does It Mean?

Find a word in the story that means...

1. very nice looking   _____

2. thickly covered in hair _____

3. thinking too well of yourself _____

4. strong   _____

5. very upset   _____

6. smart   _____

7. told how to do something _____

8. silly   _____

~~~~~~ Adjectives ~~~~~~

Adjectives are words that describe. Circle the adjectives in these phrases.

1. (long) (furry) tail   4. big, tasty fish

2. large, powerful paws   5. cold, smooth ice

3. long, sharp claws   6. small, bare stump

Write three adjectives that describe you.

_____   _____   _____

The Sounds of y

Write the sound made by the letter **y** at the end of each word.

my—i   furry—e

1. angry _____   7. try _____

2. cry _____   8. very _____

3. fly _____   9. hungry _____

4. many _____   10. why _____

5. funny _____   11. shy _____

6. silly _____   12. buy _____

What sound of **y** do you usually hear
at the end of a one-syllable word? _____

What sound of **y** do you usually hear
at the end of a two-syllable word? _____

Sh, Wh, Ch, Th

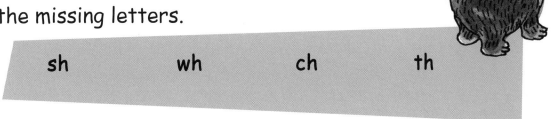

Fill in the missing letters.

sh	wh	ch	th

1. Bear **th**ought his tail was handsome.

2. Marcos used a _____arp hook to catch the fi_____.

3. One _____eel on his wagon is broken.

4. Do you have an apple for lun_____?

5. Mo_____er said, "You may make a sandwi_____ if you want a snack."

Syllables

How many syllables are in these words?

fish—1	furry—2	powerful—3

1. bear _**1**_   5. fox _____   9. pretended _____

2. other _____   6. tail _____   10. handsome _____

3. winter _____   7. used _____   11. laughing _____

4. passed _____   8. animal _____   12. surrounded _____

Bear

Draw and color the other side of this big bear.

Write a funny story about this bear.

_____

_____

_____

_____

_____

A Visit to the Monterey Bay Aquarium

Every Sunday afternoon, Neno and his father go somewhere together. His father always takes Neno to great places. Today they are going to the aquarium.

The giant kelp grows very fast.

Neno and his father stood in front of a huge tank. In the tank was the tallest water plant Neno had ever seen. "That's giant kelp," his dad said. "It's a kind of seaweed."

All kinds of fishes were swimming in and out of the giant kelp. Large schools of silver fish swam past. All of a sudden, the fish would turn and swim the other way.

There were sharks in the tank, too. "Won't the sharks eat the other fish?" asked Neno.

"No," answered his father. "The sharks are kept well fed. They don't need to eat the other fish."

A leopard shark swims in the tank.

Next they walked over to the otter tank. The otters swam around the tank. Sometimes they rolled over in the water. It looked like they were having fun.

It was feeding time for the otters, too. Their keeper was throwing bits of crab, squid, and fish into the water. The hungry otters swam after the food as it fell to the bottom of the tank.

"I wish I could pet an otter," said Neno.

"You can't pet them," said Father, "but you can touch otter fur."

The sea otter plays in the tank.

Neno followed his father to a table nearby. The guide at the table handed Neno a piece of otter fur. "Wow! This is the softest thing I've ever touched," Neno said.

"An otter's fur helps keep it warm and dry in cold water," explained the guide.

"I know a place where you can touch living sea animals," said Father.

"All right!" said Neno as he followed his father. He saw some kids standing around an open tank. He hurried over to see what was going on.

Soon Neno was touching a sea star.

The guide showed Neno sea stars.

The guide showed Neno sea stars that were different sizes and colors. Some were smooth and some were bumpy. "I thought they all had five arms," said Neno.

mouth

tube feet

Underside of a sea star

"A lot of people think that," said the guide. "There are all kinds of sea stars. Look carefully as you go around the aquarium. You might see a huge one with many arms."

Neno thanked the guide and followed his father.

"Let's go to the kelp lab," said Father. "We can take a closer look at a sea star there."

A magnified look at one ray of a sea star

Neno and his father stopped at many tanks. Each tank had interesting animals to look at.

As they went upstairs, Neno said, "Wow! I didn't know there were so many kinds of sea animals here."

"Can you remember what you saw?" asked Father.

Neno listed the animals for his father. "I saw...

Sea anemones wave their tentacles.

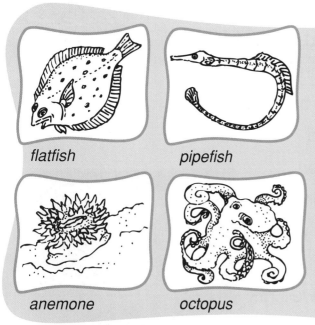

flatfish *pipefish*

anemone *octopus*

flatfish with their eyes sticking out of the sand,

pipefish hiding in sea grass,

anemones that look like flowers,

and a giant octopus moving around the rocks.

"I really like the octopus. I want to go back and look at it again. And I want to see the birds, too."

"We don't have time to do that today. We will come back another time," said Father.

Reading • EMC 4530 • ©2005 by Evan-Moor Corp.

Then Neno and his father hurried over to take a quick look at the penguins. The penguins were fun to watch. They jumped into the water and swam with their paddle-like wings.

They stopped to take a funny picture of Neno sitting in a giant clam shell. "This will be a great picture to send to your grandparents," said Father.

Next it was time to go to Father's favorite place. They rode up an escalator. Then they walked up to a huge tank. In the tank were beautiful jellies. The jellies were moving slowly through the water.

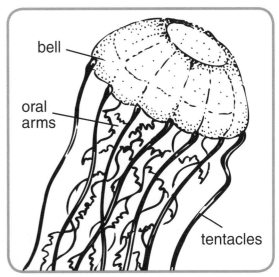

Some jellies' tentacles can be up to twelve feet long.

In the next room was another huge tank. Here were many kinds of big fish. "Look at that huge fish," said Father. He pointed at the strangest fish Neno had ever seen. "That's a sunfish," explained Father.

Sunfish (mola mola)

"It looks like it's all head," laughed Neno.

Next they went outside to look at the big tide pool for a few minutes. A friendly guide told Neno the names of the birds and animals that were in the tide pool.

Neno looked through a telescope. He saw sea lions and seals resting on rocks. He saw an otter wrapped up in kelp. He saw people in kayaks and sailboats.

Neno looked up at his father, smiled, and said, "This was great! Thank you for bringing me here today."

This story was about a visit to the Monterey Bay Aquarium in Monterey, California. (montereybayaquarium.org)

Answer Questions about
A Visit to the
Monterey Bay
Aquarium

Fill in the circle or write the answer.

1. What is an aquarium?

_____

_____

2. Why did Neno like going places with his father?

_____

3. Why don't the sharks eat the other fish in the tank?

   ○ They can't catch the other fish.

   ○ They are fed other food.

   ○ Sharks don't eat.

4. Where could kids touch live animals?

   ○ in the big tide pool

   ○ in the ocean

   ○ in the open tank

5. List three things you learned about otters.

_____

_____

_____

What Neno Saw

List these animals that Neno saw in alphabetical order.

shark	otter	seal
pipefish	jellies	anemone
penguin	flatfish	octopus
sunfish		

1. _____

2. _____

3. _____

4. _____

5. _____

6. _____

7. _____

8. _____

9. _____

10. _____

Reading • EMC 4530 • ©2005 by Evan-Moor Corp.

Aquarium Crossword Puzzle

aquarium	diver	fish	kelp
octopus	otter	sea star	shark

Across

2.

5.

6.

7.

Down

1.

2.

3.

4.

The Sounds of g

Read the words.
Write the sound the letter g makes (g or j).

1. go   _g_   5. gobble   _____

2. gem   _____   6. giant   _____

3. garden   _____   7. giraffe   _____

4. gingerbread _____   8. goat   _____

A Word Family

ark

Write **ark** on each line to make a word family.
Read the new words to an adult.

b_____   p_____   sh_____

d_____   l_____   m_____

Write sentences using two of your new words.

1. _____

   _____

2. _____

   _____

Words That Sound the Same

Circle the correct word.

1. Sharks swim in the _____. | see (sea)

2. Did you _____ the shark? | see sea

3. The wind _____ his hat away. | blew blue

4. White clouds were in the _____ sky. | blew blue

5. An octopus has _____ tentacles. | ate eight

6. The octopus _____ some shrimp. | ate eight

7. A fish swam _____ the children. | by buy

8. Are you going to _____ your lunch? | by buy

9. How much do you _____? | way weigh

10. Which _____ is the aquarium? | way weigh

In the Deep Blue Ocean

Circle the names of animals that live in the ocean.

octopus	sunfish
flatfish	spider
horse	sea star
anemone	crab
elephant	parrot
caterpillar	shark
jellies	whale
sea snail	lobster

Reading • EMC 4530 • ©2005 by Evan-Moor Corp.

Tracking Form

Topic	Color in each page you complete.					
Happy Birthday, Lee!	6	7	8	9	10	11
My Dog Max	15	16	17	18	19	20
Five Furry Kittens	22	23				
Camping	27	28	29	30	31	32
Peanut Butter	35	36	37	38	39	40
The Case of the Missing Apples	44	45	46	47	48	49
May I Keep Her?	53	54	55	56	57	58
Rashma's Nest	62	63	64	65	66	67
Ten Little Monkeys	69	70				
Pancakes Every Sunday	74	75	76	77	78	79
Row Your Boat	85	86	87	88	89	90
The Ugly Duckling	96	97	98	99	100	101
Elephants	105	106	107	108	109	110
How Bear Lost His Tail	115	116	117	118	119	120
A Visit to the Monterey Bay Aquarium	127	128	129	130	131	132

Answer Key

Checking your child's work is an important part of learning. It allows you to see what your child knows well and what areas need more practice. It also provides an opportunity for you to help your child understand that making mistakes is a part of learning.

When an error is discovered, ask your child to look carefully at the question or problem. Errors often occur through misreading. Your child can quickly correct these errors. Help your child with items she or he finds difficult.

The answer key pages can be used in several ways:

- Remove the answer pages and give the book to your child. Go over the answers as each story and the accompanying activity pages are completed.

- Leave the answer pages in the book and give the practice pages to your child one story unit at a time.

Page 6

Page 7

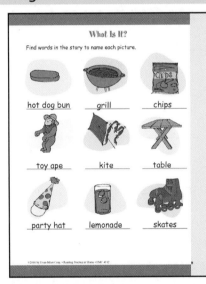

Page 8

Page 9

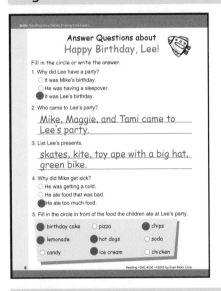

Page 10

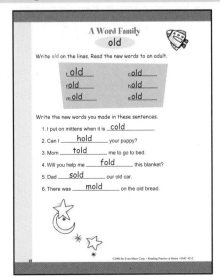

Page 11

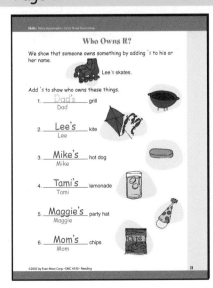

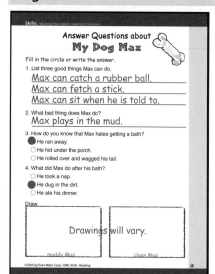

Page 15

Skills: Recalling Story Details; Drawing Conclusions

Answer Questions about My Dog Max

Fill in the circle or write the answer.

1. List three good things Max can do.
   Max can catch a rubber ball.
   Max can fetch a stick.
   Max can sit when he is told to.

2. What bad thing does Max do?
   Max plays in the mud.

3. How do you know that Max hates getting a bath?
   ● He ran away.
   ○ He hid under the porch.
   ○ He rolled over and wagged his tail.

4. What did Max do after his bath?
   ○ He took a nap.
   ● He dug in the dirt.
   ○ He ate his dinner.

Draw.

Drawings will vary.

muddy Max   clean Max

©2005 by Evan-Moor Corp. • EMC 4530 • Reading

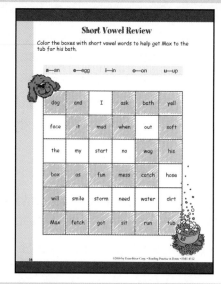

Page 16

Short Vowel Review

Color the boxes with short vowel words to help get Max to the tub for his bath.

a—an   e—egg   i—in   o—on   u—up

dog	and	I	ask	bath	yell
face	it	mud	when	out	soft
the	my	start	no	wag	his
box	as	fun	mess	catch	hose
will	smile	storm	need	water	dirt
Max	fetch	got	sit	run	tub

©2000 by Evan-Moor Corp. • Reading Practice at Home • EMC 4512

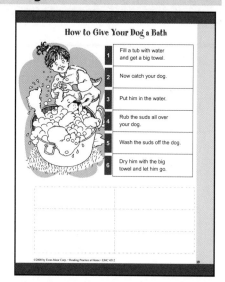

Page 17

How to Give Your Dog a Bath

1	Fill a tub with water and get a big towel.
2	Now catch your dog.
3	Put him in the water.
4	Rub the suds all over your dog.
5	Wash the suds off the dog.
6	Dry him with the big towel and let him go.

©2000 by Evan-Moor Corp. • Reading Practice at Home • EMC 4512

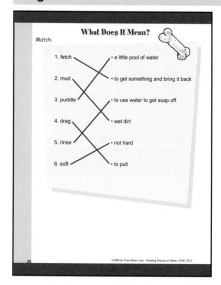

Page 18

What Does It Mean?

Match.

1. fetch — to get something and bring it back
2. mud — wet dirt
3. puddle — a little pool of water
4. drag — to pull
5. rinse — to use water to get soap off
6. soft — not hard

©2000 by Evan-Moor Corp. • Reading Practice at Home • EMC 4512

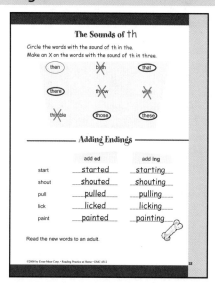

Page 19

The Sounds of th

Circle the words with the sound of th in the.
Make an X on the words with the sound of th in three.

(then)   ba⊗h   (that)
(there)   thr⊗w   wi⊗h
thi⊗ble   (those)   (these)

Adding Endings

	add ed	add ing
start	started	starting
shout	shouted	shouting
pull	pulled	pulling
lick	licked	licking
paint	painted	painting

Read the new words to an adult.

©2000 by Evan-Moor Corp. • Reading Practice at Home • EMC 4512

Page 20

Skills: Using Pronouns

Pronouns

Pronouns are words that take the place of nouns.

he   his   she   her   him

Write a pronoun on each line.

1. Jan has a great dog.
   She has a great dog.

2. Max can catch a ball.
   He can catch a ball.

3. Jan's dog was a muddy mess.
   Her dog was a muddy mess.

4. Jan pushed and pulled Max.
   She pushed and pulled Max.

5. Jan gave Max a bath.
   She gave him a bath.

6. Jan put the tub and towel away.
   She put the tub and towel away.

7. Max was digging in the dirt.
   He was digging in the dirt.

8. Max licked Jan's face.
   He licked her face.

Sharpen Your Skills—Reading—EMC 9726 • © Evan-Moor Corp.

Page 22

Skills: Recalling Story Details; Identifying Rhyming Words; Using Words for Ordinal Numbers

Answer Questions about Five Furry Kittens

Fill in the circle or write the answer.

1. Why were the kittens sitting?
   ○ In a tree
   ○ on the ground
   ● on the fence

2. What were the kittens doing?
   first   danced on her toes
   fifth   sang a song
   second   washed his little black nose
   fourth   jumped down to the ground
   third   turned around and around

3. Find the words in the poem that rhyme with these words.
   sight   night
   around   ground
   long   song
   nose   toes

Reading • EMC 4530 • ©2005 by Evan-Moor Corp.

Page 23

Words That Mean the Same

Match the words that mean the same.

little — quick
grin — yell
fast — smile
shout — small

middle — glad
happy — slow
pokey — center
large — big

Colorful Kittens

Color the kittens.

first yellow   fourth gray   third black   fifth orange   second brown

The kittens should be colored correctly.

©2000 by Evan-Moor Corp. • Reading Practice at Home • EMC 4512

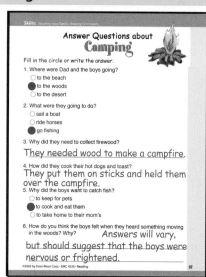

Page 27

Skills: Recalling Story Details; Drawing Conclusions

Answer Questions about Camping

Fill in the circle or write the answer.

1. Where were Dad and the boys going?
   ○ to the beach
   ● to the woods
   ○ to the desert

2. What were they going to do?
   ○ sail a boat
   ○ ride horses
   ● go fishing

3. Why did they need to collect firewood?
   They needed wood to make a campfire.

4. How did they cook their hot dogs and toast?
   They put them on sticks and held them over the campfire.

5. Why did the boys want to catch fish?
   ○ to keep for pets
   ● to cook and eat them
   ○ to take home to their mom's

6. How do you think the boys felt when they heard something moving in the woods? Why? Answers will vary, but should suggest that the boys were nervous or frightened.

©2005 by Evan-Moor Corp. • EMC 4530 • Reading

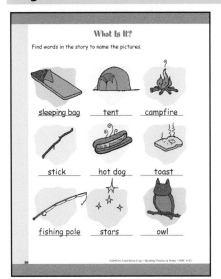

What Is It?

Find words in the story to name the pictures.

sleeping bag | tent | campfire

stick | hot dog | toast

fishing pole | stars | owl

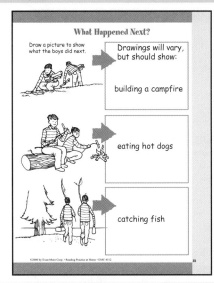

What Happened Next?

Draw a picture to show what the boys did next.

Drawings will vary, but should show:

building a campfire

eating hot dogs

catching fish

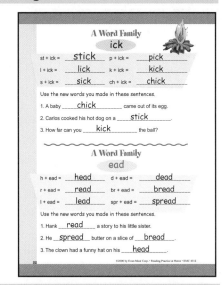

A Word Family
ick

st + ick = stick | p + ick = pick
l + ick = lick | k + ick = kick
s + ick = sick | ch + ick = chick

Use the new words you made in these sentences.

1. A baby chick came out of its egg.
2. Carlos cooked his hot dog on a stick.
3. How far can you kick the ball?

A Word Family
ead

h + ead = head | d + ead = dead
r + ead = read | br + ead = bread
l + ead = lead | spr + ead = spread

Use the new words you made in these sentences.

1. Hank read a story to his little sister.
2. He spread butter on a slice of bread.
3. The clown had a funny hat on his head.

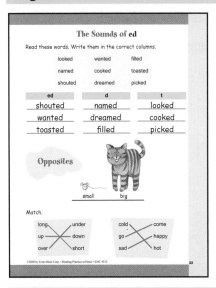

The Sounds of ed

Read these words. Write them in the correct columns.

looked | wanted | filled
named | cooked | toasted
shouted | dreamed | picked

ed	d	t
shouted	named	looked
wanted	dreamed	cooked
toasted	filled	picked

Opposites

small | big

Match.

long — under
up — down
over — short

cold — come
go — happy
sad — hot

What Are You Doing?

Words that tell what you are doing are called verbs.

Draw a circle around the doing words (verbs).

camping | campfire | stars
sleeping | cooked | moving
scary | firewood | crawled
fishing | sang | good
funny | told | peanut butter
marshmallows | bright | dreaming

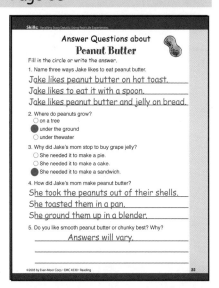

Skills: Recalling Story Details Using Real-Life Experiences

Answer Questions about
Peanut Butter

Fill in the circle or write the answer.

1. Name three ways Jake likes to eat peanut butter.
Jake likes peanut butter on hot toast.
Jake likes to eat it with a spoon.
Jake likes peanut butter and jelly on bread.

2. Where do peanuts grow?
○ on a tree
● under the ground
○ under the water

3. Why did Jake's mom stop to buy grape jelly?
○ She needed it to make a pie.
○ She needed it to make a cake.
● She needed it to make a sandwich.

4. How did Jake's mom make peanut butter?
She took the peanuts out of their shells.
She toasted them in a pan.
She ground them up in a blender.

5. Do you like smooth peanut butter or chunky best? Why?
Answers will vary.

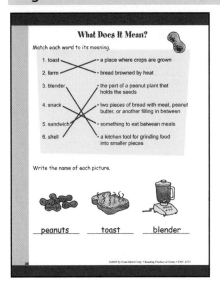

What Does It Mean?

Match each word to its meaning.

1. toast — a place where crops are grown
2. farm — bread browned by heat
3. blender — the part of a peanut plant that holds the seeds
4. snack — two pieces of bread with meat, peanut butter, or another filling in between
5. sandwich — something to eat between meals
6. shell — a kitchen tool for grinding food into smaller pieces

Write the name of each picture.

peanuts | toast | blender

A Peanut Butter Sandwich

Number the sentences to show how to make a peanut butter sandwich.

6 Cut the sandwich in half.
1 Get out the bread, peanut butter, jelly, and a knife.
5 Put the slices of bread together.
4 Put a lot of jelly on the other slice of bread.
7 Sit down and eat it up!
2 Open the jars of peanut butter and jelly.
3 Put a lot of peanut butter on one slice of bread.

Make an X on the peanut butter sandwich you would like to eat.

Answers will vary.

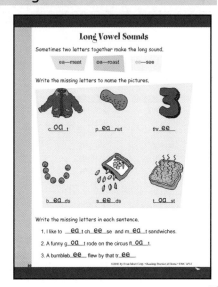

Long Vowel Sounds

Sometimes two letters together make the long sound.

ea—meat | oa—roast | ee—see

Write the missing letters to name the pictures.

c oa t | p ea nut | thr ee

b ea ds | s ee ds | t oa st

Write the missing letters in each sentence.

1. I like to ea t ch ee se and m ea t sandwiches.
2. A funny g oa t rode on the circus fl oa t.
3. A bumbleb ee flew by that tr ee.

Page 39

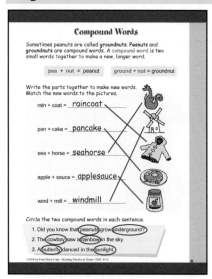

Compound Words

Sometimes peanuts are called **groundnuts**. Peanuts and **groundnuts** are compound words. A compound word is two small words together to make a new, longer word.

| pea + nut = peanut | ground + nut = groundnut |

Write the parts together to make new words. Match the new words to the pictures.

rain + coat = **raincoat**

pan + cake = **pancake**

sea + horse = **seahorse**

apple + sauce = **applesauce**

wind + mill = **windmill**

Circle the two compound words in each sentence.
1. Did you know that (peanuts) grow (underground?)
2. The (cowboy) saw a (rainbow) in the sky.
3. A (butterfly) danced in the (sunlight.)

Page 40

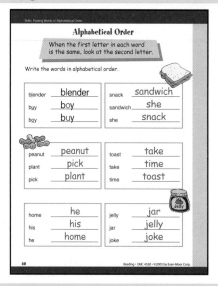

Alphabetical Order

When the first letter in each word is the same, look at the second letter.

Write the words in alphabetical order.

blender	**blender**		snack	**sandwich**
buy	**boy**		sandwich	**she**
boy	**buy**		she	**snack**

peanut	**peanut**		toast	**take**
plant	**pick**		take	**time**
pick	**plant**		time	**toast**

home	**he**		jelly	**jar**
his	**his**		jar	**jelly**
he	**home**		joke	**joke**

Page 44

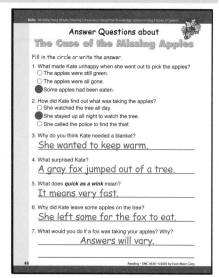

Answer Questions about
The Case of the Missing Apples

Fill in the circle or write the answer.
1. What made Kate unhappy when she went out to pick the apples?
   ○ The apples were still green.
   ○ The apples were all gone.
   ● Some apples had been eaten.

2. How did Kate find out what was taking the apples?
   ○ She watched the tree all day.
   ● She stayed up all night to watch the tree.
   ○ She called the police to find the thief.

3. Why do you think Kate needed a blanket?
   She wanted to keep warm.

4. What surprised Kate?
   A gray fox jumped out of a tree.

5. What does **quick as a wink** mean?
   It means very fast.

6. Why did Kate leave some apples on the tree?
   She left some for the fox to eat.

7. What would you do if a fox was taking your apples? Why?
   Answers will vary.

Page 45

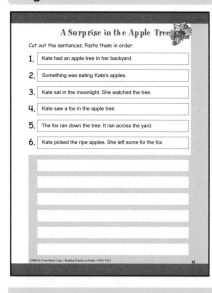

A Surprise in the Apple Tree

Cut out the sentences. Paste them in order.

1. Kate had an apple tree in her backyard.
2. Something was eating Kate's apples.
3. Kate sat in the moonlight. She watched the tree.
4. Kate saw a fox in the apple tree.
5. The fox ran down the tree. It ran across the yard.
6. Kate picked the ripe apples. She left some for the fox.

Page 46

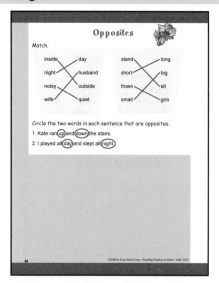

Opposites

Match.

inside — day
night — husband
noisy — outside
wife — quiet

stand — long
short — big
frown — sit
small — grin

Circle the two words in each sentence that are opposites.
1. Kate ran (up) and (down) the stairs.
2. I played all (day) and slept all (night.)

Page 47

The Sounds of gr and wr

Fill in the missing letters. Read the new words you make to an adult.

gr
grin
green
grass
grow

wr
wrap
wrong
wrist
wrestle

Use the new words you made to complete the sentences.
1. Kate started to gr**in** when she saw the fox.
2. Tom likes to wr**estle** with his brother.
3. Dad asked me to mow the gr**een** gr**ass**.
4. Can you wr**ap** this present for me?

Page 48

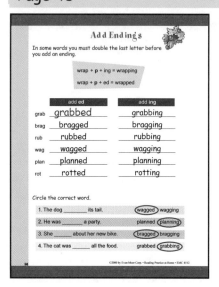

Add Endings

In some words you must double the last letter before you add an ending.

wrap + p + ing = wrapping
wrap + p + ed = wrapped

	add ed	add ing
grab	**grabbed**	**grabbing**
brag	**bragged**	**bragging**
rub	**rubbed**	**rubbing**
wag	**wagged**	**wagging**
plan	**planned**	**planning**
rot	**rotted**	**rotting**

Circle the correct word.
1. The dog _____ its tail. (wagged) wagging
2. He was _____ a party. planned (planning)
3. She _____ about her new bike. (bragged) bragging
4. The cat was _____ all the food. grabbed (grabbing)

Page 49

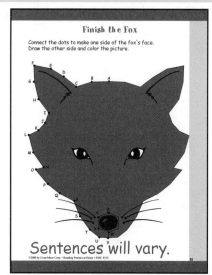

Finish the Fox

Connect the dots to make one side of the fox's face. Draw the other side and color the picture.

Sentences will vary.

Page 53

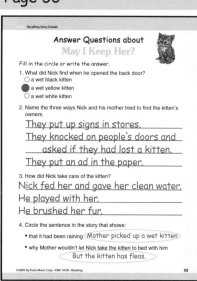

Answer Questions about
May I Keep Her?

Fill in the circle or write the answer.
1. What did Nick find when he opened the back door?
   ○ a wet black kitten
   ● a wet yellow kitten
   ○ a wet white kitten

2. Name the three ways Nick and his mother tried to find the kitten's owners.
   They put up signs in stores.
   They knocked on people's doors and asked if they had lost a kitten.
   They put an ad in the paper.

3. How did Nick take care of the kitten?
   Nick fed her and gave her clean water.
   He played with her.
   He brushed her fur.

4. Circle the sentence in the story that shows:
   • that it had been raining   (Mother picked up a wet kitten)
   • why Mother wouldn't let Nick take the kitten to bed with him
   (But the kitten has fleas.)

What Happened Next?

Pretend you are Nick. Write a letter to a friend. Tell your friend what happened after you heard the noise at the back door.

Dear _Letters will vary, but must retell events from the story._

Your friend,
Nick

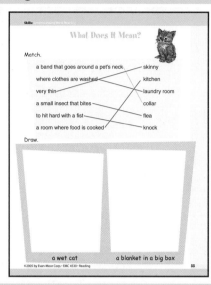

What Does It Mean?

Match.

a band that goes around a pet's neck — skinny
where clothes are washed — kitchen
very thin — laundry room
a small insect that bites — collar
to hit hard with a fist — flea
a room where food is cooked — knock

Draw.

a wet cat | a blanket in a big box

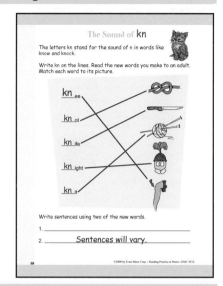

The Sound of kn

The letters kn stand for the sound of n in words like know and knock.

Write kn on the lines. Read the new words you make to an adult. Match each word to its picture.

kn_ee
kn_ot
kn_ife
kn_ight
kn_it

Write sentences using two of the new words.

1. _____
2. _____ Sentences will vary. _____

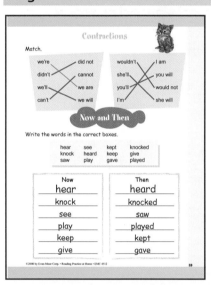

Contractions

Match.

we're — did not
didn't — cannot
we'll — we are
can't — we will

wouldn't — I am
she'll — you will
you'll — would not
I'm — she will

Now and Then

Write the words in the correct boxes.

hear   see   kept   knocked
knock   heard keep   give
saw   play   gave   played

Now	Then
hear	heard
knock	knocked
see	saw
play	played
keep	kept
give	gave

Listen for the Sound

Read the words.

night   Nick   skinny   give
kitten it   light   tried
like   his   pick   with
I   Tiger my   sign

Write each word in the correct box.

long i	short i
night	kitten
like	Nick
I	it
Tiger	his
light	skinny
my	pick
tried	give
sign	with

Answer Questions about Rashma's Nest

Fill in the circle or write the answer.

1. The robin was making a nest in _____.
   ○ a birdhouse
   ○ a hole in the ground
   ● a tree
2. The nest was made of _____.
   ○ branches and leaves
   ● twigs, weeds, and mud
   ○ grass and string
3. The robin sat on her eggs to _keep them warm_
4. The robins fed their nestlings _worms and insects_
5. Rashma felt _sad_ when the birds flew away.
6. Rashma's brother told her that the birds _had to be off doing bird things_

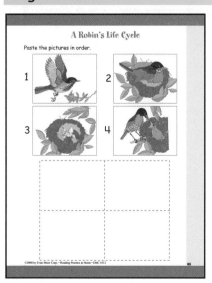

A Robin's Life Cycle

Paste the pictures in order.

1   2
3   4

What Is It?

Find words in the story to name these pictures.

robin
worm
beak
nestling
insect or ant

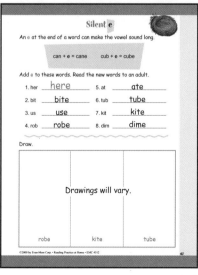

Silent e

An e at the end of a word can make the vowel sound long.

can + e = cane   cub + e = cube

Add e to these words. Read the new words to an adult.

1. her _here_   5. at _ate_
2. bit _bite_   6. tub _tube_
3. us _use_   7. kit _kite_
4. rob _robe_   8. dim _dime_

Draw.

Drawings will vary.

robe | kite | tube

More Than One

Add s. bird—birds		Change y to i and add es. cherry—cherries	
1. robin	**robins**	5. berry	**berries**
2. feather	**feathers**	6. nest	**nests**
3. baby	**babies**	7. penny	**pennies**
4. egg	**eggs**	8. pony	**ponies**

They or Them? Write they or them on the line.

1. Rashma and her brother saw the birds.

They saw the birds.

2. The robins fed worms to the nestlings.

The robins fed worms to **them**.

3. What did the nestlings look like?

What did **they** look like?

4. Rashma didn't want the birds to go.

Rashma didn't want **them** to go.

©2000 by Evan-Moor Corp. • Reading Practice at Home • EMC 4512

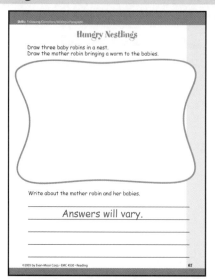

Skills: Following Directions/Writing a Paragraph

Hungry Nestlings

Draw three baby robins in a nest.
Draw the mother robin bringing a worm to the babies.

Write about the mother robin and her babies.

Answers will vary.

©2005 by Evan-Moor Corp. • EMC 4530 • Reading

Answer Questions about Ten Little Monkeys

Fill in the circle or write the correct answer.
Write the correct number word.

1. How many monkeys were...

splashing in the sea? **two** wearing funny hats? **eight**

digging with a spade? **six** nodding little heads? **nine**

swinging in a tree? **one**

2. What were seven monkeys doing?
○ nodding little heads
○ wearing funny hats
● chasing furry cats

3. What were three monkeys doing?
○ sleeping in their beds
● playing on a swing
○ swinging in a tree

Draw a monkey sleeping in this bed.

©2005 by Evan-Moor Corp. • EMC 4530 • Reading

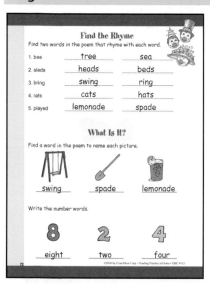

Find the Rhyme

Find two words in the poem that rhyme with each word.

1. bee	**tree**	**sea**
2. sleds	**heads**	**beds**
3. bring	**swing**	**ring**
4. rats	**cats**	**hats**
5. played	**lemonade**	**spade**

What Is It?

Find a word in the poem to name each picture.

swing   **spade**   **lemonade**

Write the number words.

8 **eight**   2 **two**   4 **four**

©2000 by Evan-Moor Corp. • Reading Practice at Home • EMC 4512

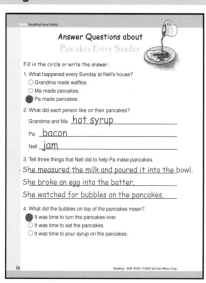

Skills: Recalling Story Details

Answer Questions about Pancakes Every Sunday

Fill in the circle or write the answer.

1. What happened every Sunday at Nell's house?
○ Grandma made waffles.
○ Ma made pancakes.
● Pa made pancakes.

2. What did each person like on their pancakes?

Grandma and Ma **hot syrup**

Pa **bacon**

Nell **jam**

3. Tell three things that Nell did to help Pa make pancakes.

She measured the milk and poured it into the bowl.

She broke an egg into the batter.

She watched for bubbles on the pancakes.

4. What did the bubbles on top of the pancakes mean?
● It was time to turn the pancakes over.
○ It was time to eat the pancakes.
○ It was time to pour syrup on the pancakes.

Reading • EMC 4530 • ©2005 by Evan-Moor Corp.

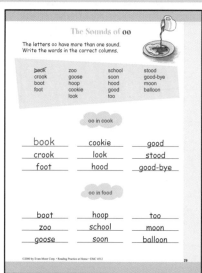

Nell's Sunday Morning

Read the sentences about Nell.
Number them in order.

5 Nell ate four pancakes.
1 Nell jumped out of bed.
3 Nell helped make the batter.
6 Nell asked for one more pancake.
4 Nell watched for bubbles on the pancakes.
2 Nell ran to the kitchen.

Number the pictures in order.

1   3   2

©2000 by Evan-Moor Corp. • Reading Practice at Home • EMC 4512

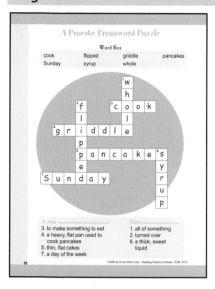

A Pancake Crossword Puzzle

Word Box

| cook | flipped | griddle | pancakes |
| Sunday | syrup | whole | |

Across
3. to make something to eat
4. a heavy, flat pan used to cook pancakes
5. thin, flat cakes
7. a day of the week

Down
1. all of something
2. turned over
6. a thick, sweet liquid

©2000 by Evan-Moor Corp. • Reading Practice at Home • EMC 4512

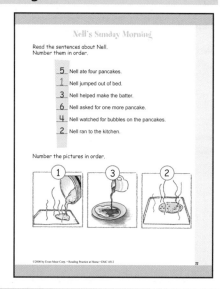

The Sounds of oo

The letters oo have more than one sound.
Write the words in the correct columns.

book	zoo	school	stood
crook	goose	soon	good-bye
boot	hoop	hood	moon
foot	cookie	good	balloon
	look	too	

oo in cook

book   **cookie**   **good**
crook   **look**   **stood**
foot   **hood**   **good-bye**

oo in food

boot   **hoop**   **too**
zoo   **school**   **moon**
goose   **soon**   **balloon**

©2000 by Evan-Moor Corp. • Reading Practice at Home • EMC 4512

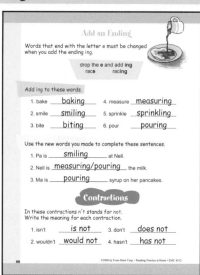

Add an Ending

Words that end with the letter e must be changed when you add the ending ing.

drop the e and add ing
race   racing

Add ing to these words.

1. bake	**baking**	4. measure	**measuring**
2. smile	**smiling**	5. sprinkle	**sprinkling**
3. bite	**biting**	6. pour	**pouring**

Use the new words you made to complete these sentences.

1. Pa is **smiling** at Nell.

2. Nell is **measuring/pouring** the milk.

3. Ma is **pouring** syrup on her pancakes.

Contractions

In these contractions n't stands for not.
Write the meaning for each contraction.

| 1. isn't | **is not** | 3. don't | **does not** |
| 2. wouldn't | **would not** | 4. hasn't | **has not** |

©2000 by Evan-Moor Corp. • Reading Practice at Home • EMC 4512

Page 79

Page 85

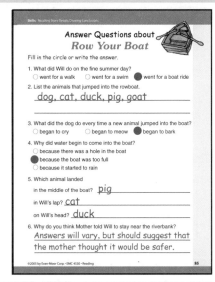

Page 86

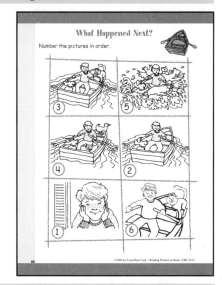

Page 87

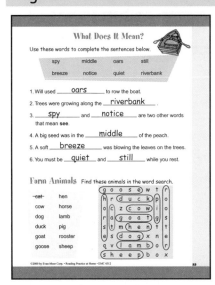

Page 88

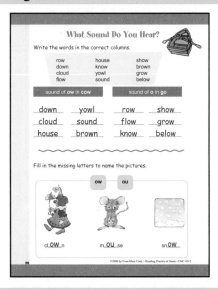

Page 89

Page 90

Page 96

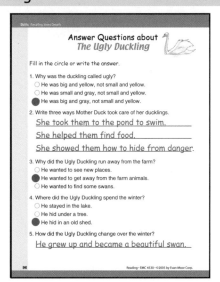

Page 97

Page 98

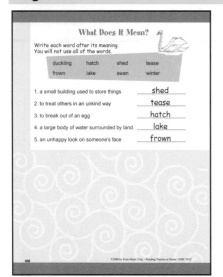

What Does It Mean?

Write each word after its meaning.
You will not use all of the words.

| duckling | hatch | shed | tease |
| frown | lake | swan | winter |

1. a small building used to store things — **shed**
2. to treat others in an unkind way — **tease**
3. to break out of an egg — **hatch**
4. a large body of water surrounded by land — **lake**
5. an unhappy look on someone's face — **frown**

Page 99

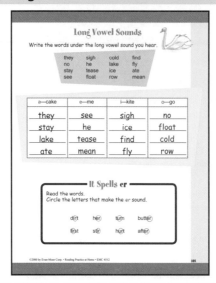

Long Vowel Sounds

Write the words under the long vowel sound you hear.

they	sigh	cold	find
no	he	lake	fly
stay	tease	ice	ate
see	float	row	mean

a—cake	e—me	i—kite	o—go
they	see	sigh	no
stay	he	ice	float
lake	tease	find	cold
ate	mean	fly	row

It Spells er

Read the words.
Circle the letters that make the er sound.

dirt   her   turn   butter
first   stir   hurt   after

Page 100

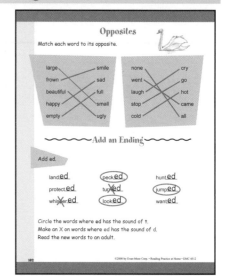

Opposites

Match each word to its opposite.

large — smile
frown — sad
beautiful — full
happy — small
empty — ugly

none — cry
went — go
laugh — hot
stop — came
cold — all

Add an Ending

Add ed.

land**ed**   peck**ed**   hunt**ed**
protect**ed**   turn**ed**   jump**ed**
whisper**ed**   look**ed**   want**ed**

Circle the words where ed has the sound of t.
Make an X on words where ed has the sound of d.
Read the new words to an adult.

Page 101

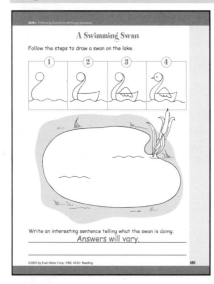

A Swimming Swan

Follow the steps to draw a swan on the lake.

Write an interesting sentence telling what the swan is doing.
Answers will vary.

Page 105

Answer Questions about Elephants

Fill in the circle or write the answer.

1. What does an elephant look like?
Answers will vary, but could include large, gray-black skin, long trunk, big ears, short hairs on back and tail.
2. Which elephants live in herds?
○ bulls and cows
● cows and calves
○ bulls and calves
3. Name two places elephants live.
Asia and Africa
4. How do elephants get their food?
They pick up their food with their trunk and put it in their mouth.
5. How else do elephants use their trunk?
They use their trunk to get food, to drink water, to catch smells in the air, and to greet each other.

Page 106

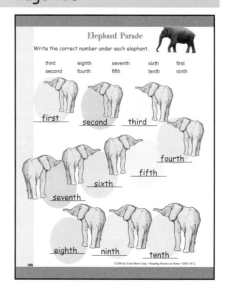

Elephant Parade

Write the correct number under each elephant.

| third | eighth | seventh | sixth | first |
| second | fourth | fifth | tenth | ninth |

first   second   third
fourth
fifth
sixth
seventh
eighth   ninth   tenth

Page 107

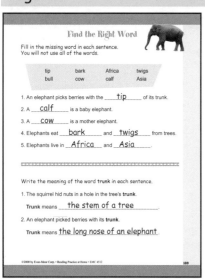

Find the Right Word

Fill in the missing word in each sentence.
You will not use all of the words.

| tip | bark | Africa | twigs |
| bull | cow | calf | Asia |

1. An elephant picks berries with the **tip** of its trunk.
2. A **calf** is a baby elephant.
3. A **cow** is a mother elephant.
4. Elephants eat **bark** and **twigs** from trees.
5. Elephants live in **Africa** and **Asia**.

Write the meaning of the word **trunk** in each sentence.

1. The squirrel hid nuts in a hole in the tree's **trunk**.
Trunk means the stem of a tree
2. An elephant picked berries with its **trunk**.
Trunk means the long nose of an elephant

Page 108

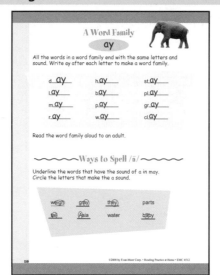

A Word Family
ay

All the words in a word family end with the same letters and sound. Write ay after each letter to make a word family.

d**ay**   h**ay**   st**ay**
l**ay**   b**ay**   pl**ay**
m**ay**   p**ay**   gr**ay**
r**ay**   w**ay**   cl**ay**

Read the word family aloud to an adult.

Ways to Spell /ā/

Underline the words that have the sound of a in may.
Circle the letters that make the a sound.

weigh   gray   they   parts
tail   Asia   water   baby

Page 109

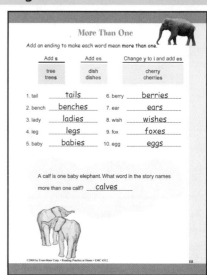

More Than One

Add an ending to make each word mean **more than one.**

Add s	Add es	Change y to i and add es
tree	dish	cherry
trees	dishes	cherries

1. tail — tails
2. bench — benches
3. lady — ladies
4. leg — legs
5. baby — babies
6. berry — berries
7. ear — ears
8. wish — wishes
9. fox — foxes
10. egg — eggs

A calf is one baby elephant. What word in the story names more than one calf? **calves**

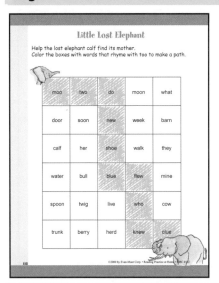

Little Lost Elephant

Help the lost elephant calf find its mother.
Color the boxes with words that rhyme with too to make a path.

moo	two	do	moon	what
door	soon	new	week	barn
calf	her	shoe	walk	they
water	bull	blue	flew	mine
spoon	twig	live	who	cow
trunk	berry	herd	knew	blue

Skills: Recalling Story Details

Answer Questions about
How BEAR Lost His TAIL

Fill in the circle or write the answer.
1. Why was Bear so proud of his tail?
○ It had brown and white stripes.
● It was long and furry.
○ It was short and curly.

2. Why were the animals afraid to make Bear angry?
He had powerful paws with sharp claws.

3. How did the clever fox trick Bear?
Fox told Bear that he could catch fish by
putting his tail in a hole in the ice.

4. What happened to Bear's long tail?
○ It grew longer and longer.
● It froze and broke off.
○ The fish ate Bear's tail off.

Draw Bear with a long, handsome, bushy tail.
Draw Bear with a short stump of a tail.

Drawings will vary.

What Happened Next?

Draw what happened next.

As Bear was looking for something to eat, he passed the river.
What happened next?
Drawings will vary, but should show:
Bear watching or talking to Fox.

Fox told Bear he had caught fish by putting his tail in a hole in the ice.
What happened next?
Bear digging in the ice with his claws.

Bear fell asleep with his tail in the water. The water froze.
What happened next?
Bear looking at his stub of a tail.

What Does It Mean?

Find a word in the story that means...

1. very nice looking — handsome
2. thickly covered in hair — furry
3. thinking too well of yourself — proud
4. strong — powerful
5. very upset — angry
6. smart — clever
7. told how to do something — explained
8. silly — foolish

Adjectives

Adjectives are words that describe. Circle the adjectives in these phrases.
1. long furry tail
2. large powerful paws
3. long sharp claws
4. big tasty fish
5. cold smooth ice
6. small bare stump

Write three adjectives that describe you.
Answers will vary.

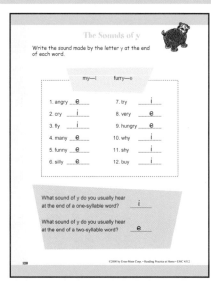

The Sounds of y

Write the sound made by the letter y at the end of each word.

my—i   furry—e

1. angry _e_   7. try _i_
2. cry _i_   8. very _e_
3. fly _i_   9. hungry _e_
4. many _e_   10. why _i_
5. funny _e_   11. shy _i_
6. silly _e_   12. buy _i_

What sound of y do you usually hear at the end of a one-syllable word? _i_

What sound of y do you usually hear at the end of a two-syllable word? _e_

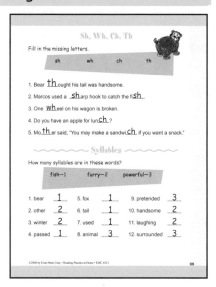

Sh, Wh, Ch, Th

Fill in the missing letters.

sh   wh   ch   th

1. Bear **th**ought his tail was handsome.
2. Marcos used a **sh**arp hook to catch the fi**sh**.
3. One **wh**eel on his wagon is broken.
4. Do you have an apple for lun**ch**?
5. Mo**th**er said, "You may make a sandwi**ch** if you want a snack."

Syllables

How many syllables are in these words?

fish—1   furry—2   powerful—3

1. bear _1_   5. fox _1_   9. pretended _3_
2. other _2_   6. tail _1_   10. handsome _2_
3. winter _2_   7. used _1_   11. laughing _2_
4. passed _1_   8. animal _3_   12. surrounded _3_

Skills: Following Directions; Writing a Story

Bear

Draw and color the other side of this big bear.

Write a funny story about this bear.
Answers will vary.

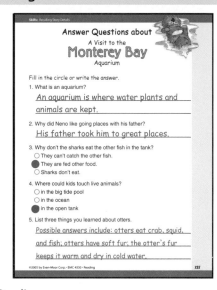

Skills: Recalling Story Details

Answer Questions about
A Visit to the
Monterey Bay
Aquarium

Fill in the circle or write the answer.
1. What is an aquarium?
An aquarium is where water plants and
animals are kept.

2. Why did Neno like going places with his father?
His father took him to great places.

3. Why don't the sharks eat the other fish in the tank?
○ They can't catch the other fish.
● They are fed other food.
○ Sharks don't eat.

4. Where could kids touch live animals?
○ in the big tide pool
○ in the ocean
● in the open tank

5. List three things you learned about otters.
Possible answers include: otters eat crab, squid,
and fish; otters have soft fur; the otter's fur
keeps it warm and dry in cold water.

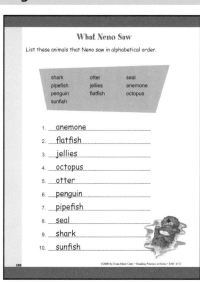

What Neno Saw

List these animals that Neno saw in alphabetical order.

shark   otter   seal
pipefish   jellies   anemone
penguin   flatfish   octopus
sunfish

1. anemone
2. flatfish
3. jellies
4. octopus
5. otter
6. penguin
7. pipefish
8. seal
9. shark
10. sunfish

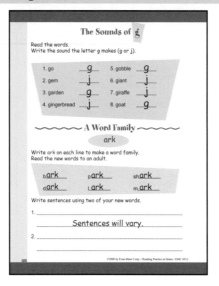

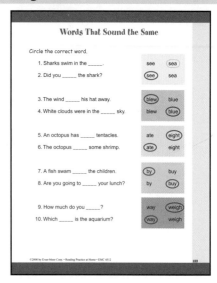